# Cat
## Be Good

A
Commonsense
Approach
to
Training
Your Cat

**Annie Bruce**

Foreword by Dr. J. Douglas Courtley, D.V.M.

Cover and book design by David Levine Design

Sidebar Illustrations by James Riddle

All other illustrations by Sara Levine

Cover photo by Corbis/Julie Houck ©

Printed in the United States of America

First printing January, 2000

**Disclaimer:** The information in this book is not meant to take the place of medical advice or expert veterinary care. Consult a veterinarian when there is a possibility that your cat is ill.

**Cataloging-in-Publication Data**

Bruce, Annie, 1955-

      Cat Be Good : A Commonsense Approach to Training Your Cat / by Annie Bruce.
          p. cm.
      Includes index.
      ISBN 0-9674062-0-X  :  $15.00
      1. Cats—Behavior.  2. Cats—Psychology.  3. Animal behavior.
4. Pets—Care.
I. Title.

SF446.5        2000

636.8
Library of Congress Catalog Card Number 99-94833

*This book is dedicated—*

to those who have been
    sick,
        abused,
            abandoned,
                forgotten.

in memory of my wonderful mother and father.

to Bruce, Sherri, Constance, Catalina, David,
    Emillia and Sarah Jane.

And in special memory of Moses.
May the slavery end.

Love,

*Annie Bruce*

# TABLE OF CONTENTS

# FOREWORD

As a practicing veterinarian for the past 29 years, I have had numerous clients come to me for advice regarding their cat's behavior problems and health concerns. Annie addresses some innovative approaches for dealing with some typical, behavior problems and health issues. Annie educates cat owners in an easy-to-read dialog for common, everyday problems most cat owners face. She says it in words that are easy to understand, using techniques that don't require a lot of work or money. *Cat Be Good* is a great, practical book for understanding and modifying your cat's behavior.

Many people view cats as nonverbal and don't expect them to obey commands, but *Cat Be Good* breaks-through communication barriers. Annie treats cat behavior, and intelligence, in ways that have typically been accredited to dogs. Cats *can* be trained by using words and commands instead of clickers or squirt bottles. Annie also addresses the topic of how health problems may be the cause of destructive behavior. Also included in *Cat Be Good* are guidelines for determining when your cat needs veterinarian help, scratching post training, teaching your cat to come when called, and much more. Annie demonstrates that cats are trainable.

*Cat Be Good* is a wonderful, all-around commonsense guide for living with cats. I think that *Cat Be Good* would be an excellent addition to any cat owner's library, a helpful guide for both new and long-time cat owners.

Dr. J. Douglas Courtley, D.V.M.
Niwot Veterinary Clinic
Niwot, Colorado

Sara E. Levine

# Cat Basics

# INTRODUCTION

*Mistakes are at the very base of human thought, . . .*
*feeding the structure like root nodules. If we were not*
*provided with the knack of being wrong, we could*
*never get anything useful done.*

—LEWIS THOMAS

The day my cat Simon attacked me was the day I really started learning about cats. It was a hot August day in Detroit. I was 15 years old and playing rough with my cat, Simon. He wasn't neutered—back then, most males weren't. And I made the mistake of thinking my three-year-old cat would never, could never hurt me.

Simon was becoming agitated from my rough handling of him. I ignored the swish of his tail, his hunched back and his heavy breathing, and continued to wrestle with him. After I quit and walked away, I turned around and saw Simon's angry glare. He leapt and flew across the room at me, tore into my right arm with all fours, and sank his teeth deep into my bicep. The violence left me stunned and terribly injured. I couldn't use my arm for over a month. That's what just *one* bite from a cat can do.

I'd had cats for six years by then, and did not realize their potential. For a few days, I thought about getting rid of Simon but since I had provoked him that hardly seemed fair. Eventually I worked through my fear and Simon remained a good friend and never hurt me again. When he was nine, he got lost for 13 months before he found his way back home. He was a great cat!

Ever since, I've been learning about cats, frequently through mistakes. I have found things that work, and things that don't. I've learned how to have cats who don't tear up our fine carpet and furniture and who listen to what I tell them—without my having to do much work or spend much money. I'd rather spend money on fun stuff or cat toys than on cat doctors or home repairs.

Now, after owning and learning about cats for 35 years, I find myself a cat behaviorist. Actually, I call myself a "cat owner consultant" because I am expert at being a cat owner now and my primary goal is to help the *owner*. There are a lot of outdated beliefs, bad advice, and convincing advertising for bad products out there. Using a squirt bottle is just one example. And it's both the cat and the owner who will pay, sometimes dearly, for being misinformed.

I wrote this book so that you will not only have cats but that you'll have *good* cats, for a very long time. You'll see! Cats do listen and they will learn. Cats aren't really mysterious—as we have been led to believe. As you'll soon find out your cat can be good.

*Annie Bruce*

# THE TRUTH ABOUT CATS

*It always gives me a shiver when I see a
cat seeing what I can't see.*

—ELEANOR FARJEON

Cats have acquired an undeserved reputation for being untrainable. But nothing could be farther from the truth. Cats are smart. And trainable. Many people assume that cats are antisocial and unattached. This is *not* true. Some believe that cats are loners, and think nothing of leaving a cat alone for long periods of time. Cats shouldn't be left alone any more than people, dogs or birds should. The truth is, cats *hunt* alone and prefer company the rest of the time.

## A PARADE OF MYTHS

Below are just a few myths that have caused misfortune to many cats. Many cat myths have begun only in the last few decades.

- ✘ Cats are unsociable and never get lonely
- ✘ Cats always land on their feet
- ✘ Cats aren't trainable (or, they don't listen)
- ✘ Indoor cats must be declawed
- ✘ Declawing saves time and money
- ✘ Cats do not like their paws touched
- ✘ Spanking a cat is effective punishment
- ✘ Diet and exercise aren't important to cats
- ✘ Black cats are bad luck

## ANNIE'S BASIC CAT SECRET

This book is all about my one simple secret to cat behavior. I call it the ABCs of cat behavior (Annie's Basic Cat Secret):

### *"CATS ARE LIKE PEOPLE."*

## CATS ARE LIKE PEOPLE

There is no single strategy to behavior that is effective with every cat or person. We often need to adjust things in many aspects of our life to help our behavior.

When people are strong, healthy and confident, they don't feel threatened or intimidated by situations. When people are weak, unhealthy or insecure, they frequently behave badly.

Cats are no different. Like people, they may whine, wet the bed, be irritable or mad when they aren't feeling good.

My aim is to help you make your cat stress-tolerant, strong, confident and happy. It won't cost you much in terms of time and money. A good cat is easy to have if you know the ropes. I will teach you.

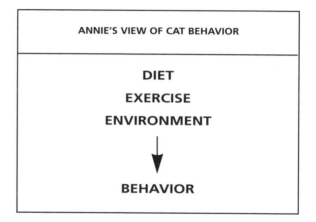

ANNIE'S VIEW OF CAT BEHAVIOR

**DIET**

**EXERCISE**

**ENVIRONMENT**

↓

**BEHAVIOR**

### BEFORE WE BEGIN

A cats' health is important to behavior. None of the advice I give in this book is intended to replace that of a veterinarian. Make sure the cat sees the veterinarian when you have any doubts about his health.

The advice in this book is tailored only to a cat that is spayed or neutered. If your cat isn't, please see the Fix 'em Good chapter.

### FERAL CATS

This book is also not meant for feral (wild) cats. It's dangerous to let a feral cat inside your house or to touch one. A feral may never learn to be part of a household. I do not recommend their adoption. There are millions of already tamed cats that will be killed this year due to lack of homes. (Alternatives for helping feral cats are listed in the appendix titled Cat Advocacy.)

## DECLAWING

Declawing is illegal or considered inhumane in several countries. It is a risky and painful procedure that amputates the claw, tendon, bone and ligament to the first knuckle of each joint. While many American veterinarians suggest declawing as a means of alleviating behavior problems such as scratching and aggression, it is, in reality, ineffective.

Declawing at first appears to save time and money. But it undermines the cat's health, confidence and attitude, and can lead to worse problems. Declawing can make a cat very expensive to own. Owners of declawed cats report higher veterinarian bills, higher repair bills and more litter box problems.

Throughout this book, I've included tips on how to offer special treatment for declawed cats. They need additional help. . . but even the best help will not make up for their loss. *Don't adopt a declawed cat and don't have one declawed.* You are better off with an able-bodied cat, not one who is permanently disabled.

## THE MAKING OF A GOOD CAT

It really doesn't take much to make a cat happy and well-behaved. The secret to cat behavior is found in these basics:

- A healthy diet
- Exercise and play
- Social interactions
- Touch
- Fresh air and sunshine
- A clean, safe toilet and bed

## SOLVING PROBLEMS

No two cases are alike so I've included lots of options. Don't feel you have to do each one but select a few since no single strategy works with every cat. Pick and choose the advice that best suits your set of circumstances. Disregard the stuff you don't think will help. If you get stuck on what to try, think of how you would solve the problem if your cat were a person.

# SAFETY

*Cats seldom make mistakes and they never make the same mistake twice.*

—CARL VAN VECHTEN

### SHOPPING LIST

✓ cat carrier
✓ curtain cleat or binder clip
✓ tattoo
✓ brightly colored, breakaway cat collar (use bell when outside)

### TRUE STORY

While cleaning the house one Tuesday morning, I heard Marvin crying loudly. I found him with his leg tangled in the pull cord of the window blinds. He could not free himself because his hind end was hanging about five inches off the floor.

When I went to grab him, he hissed at me but I was finally able to free his leg. I felt lucky that he did not get his neck caught in the cord.

Now I make sure that pull cords are inaccessible by tucking them away or wrapping them around curtain cleats.

Just as there are things to make a house safe for children, there are steps to take to protect your cats.

## CAT TOYS

Be sure to keep string and yarn inaccessible. Believe it or not, string can kill a cat. Once a cat starts swallowing string, he can't stop until he chews through it. Cats have been known to swallow very long pieces of string, yarn or ribbon, causing intestinal blockage and eventually, death. Though the image of a cat playing with a ball of yarn is a popular one, there are safer things for cats to play with.

Remove any glued-on or removable parts from toys.

## HOUSEPLANTS LOOK ENTICING BUT . . .

Cats don't understand that houseplants are not safe to eat. Poinsettias, azaleas and philodendrons are just a few poisonous and potentially deadly plants. Discourage cats from playing with any houseplants by saying "No" when they are investigating them. It also helps to keep decorative rocks on top of the soil so that cats won't be tempted to dig. Hang plants from the ceiling, beyond their reach, or find a new home for plants that are just too tempting.

## CATS DON'T ALWAYS LAND ON THEIR FEET

Open windows, balconies and rooftops are serious hazards for cats. If possible, keep these areas off-limits. If you're going to have lamps on timers, make sure the lamp is secure so that the cat can't knock the lamp over. Otherwise, the lamp is a potential fire hazard.

## DON'T WET HIM

Many people use spray bottles as a deterrent for bad behavior, but they can be dangerous. Cats are susceptible to upper respiratory infections, especially if water is forced into their mouths or noses.

## OR DRY HIM

Keep the laundry dryer door closed when unattended. Every time I close my dryer door, I look to see that no one's in there.

## BE CAREFUL OF CHEMICALS AND CLEANERS

Moth crystals or balls can destroy a cat's liver within a few hours of inhaling the fumes. Use cedar instead in closets and chests.

Keep your cats away from household cleaners. Anything dangerous for human consumption is often fatal for cats. Use baking soda, vinegar or environmentally safe natural cleaners instead of commercial cleaning products. Cats are very sensitive to chemicals, so rinse surfaces well after using any kind of cleaner.

After applying fertilizer or weed killer to the lawn, keep cats inside for the period recommended by the chemical manufacturer *and* until after the lawn has been watered. Inside the house, use roach and mouse traps instead of chemicals or poison.

## THE LITTER BOX

Avoid the use of clumping litters that contain sodium bentonite. The substance has been suspected of killing kittens. Do not keep a litter box in the garage or near the hot water heater where carbon monoxide might accumulate.

## SPEAKING OF THE GARAGE . . .

Antifreeze has been known to kill pets. Garage doors and garage door openers have killed many cats. Warm car engines are attractive on cold nights but cats are often killed when they are caught unawares beneath a car. Before starting your engine, check for cats.

 **WARNING**

**If you are pregnant, do not handle cat litter.** There is a risk of toxoplasmosis which can cause birth defects.

Note that toxoplasmosis can also be caused by eating meat that is undercooked or was improperly handled.

**Ask your doctor and your veterinarian for advice on handling cats when you're pregnant.**

## THE SEWING ROOM, OFFICE, KITCHEN, BATHROOM

Moving sewing machine needles and glimmering scissors can seriously injure cats who let curiosity get the better of them. Keep your cats away while using the machine.

Cats can swallow rubber bands and other small office supplies.

In the kitchen, toothpicks, tin foil balls, corks and cellophane can choke cats. Plastic bags can trap or suffocate.

In the bathroom, keep the toilet lid down. A thirsty cat could drink out of the bowl and get hurt by the seat falling on him or by chemicals in the toilet bowl water. Medicines meant for humans are not meant for cats, so keep them in their containers and out of reach. Aspirin and Tylenol are deadly.

## SEASONAL DANGERS

Cats will chew on, or swallow, tinsel, Christmas tree water, angel hair, Easter egg nests-all of which are toxic. Keep your cat inside during any holidays when firecrackers are used. On hot days, and even on warm days, don't leave her in the car. It only takes a few minutes in a hot car to kill your pet.

## COLLARS, HARNESSES AND LEASHES

*Any* cat who is let outside needs a collar with a phone number. Even if your cat is tattooed, he should wear a collar outdoors. Tattooed cats may be okay collarless while indoors but not outside. A bell should be used when he's outside but not inside the house or it will drive everyone, especially the cat, crazy.

Cat collars should fit loosely. Unlike dogs, cats' necks are fragile. Cats need to be able to shed the collar to avoid injury should the collar get caught in a fence. Use a breakaway collar made especially for cats. Buy brightly colored collars so you can spot him easily. Write your name on the collar with a permanent marker or include a tag.

Cats can get out of just about any harness. Use a harness or leash only while you are around to watch. Never leave your cat unattended even if he's wearing a harness.

## CAT CARRIERS

Use an airline regulation cat carrier, because they are durable, easily transportable, storable and washable. Always use a cat carrier when you travel. It is dangerous to drive with the distraction of a cat loose in a car. I once had a near accident when my cat got under the brake pedal.

## SPECIAL CONSIDERATIONS FOR DECLAWED CATS

Declawed cats are less able to respond to danger than clawed cats. Place padding in areas where they may fall since they are clumsier. Use caution when taking a declawed cat outdoors. Declawed cats can't climb trees to escape dogs and predators; they may have to fight instead of flee. Declawed cats need supervision while outside.

## DON'T LOSE HIM

The best way to permanently register ownership of your cat is to have him tattooed and the number registered with a national pet registry. It is a federal offense for any laboratory to accept a tattooed animal. And tattoos don't slip off like collars do. (See the Products and Resources appendix for details.)

You can use a new microchip implant identification method. Not just any microchip reader can decipher the chip information but most can detect that a chip is present. Shelters often carry a universal chip reader but laboratories do not. The chip is not visible and does not offer the same federal protection that tattooing does. But the chip can add protection in case your cat does get scanned.

Even with my tattooed cats, I use a collar with my phone number on it every time I take them outdoors.

Pet stores carry decals to notify firefighters how many animals are in the house. Firefighters don't have time to rescue your cats. If they see the decal, they will leave a door open for the cat to escape.

Keep a file of information about each cat in case they get lost. Please also see the Lost and Found chapter. The file should include:

- A few pictures
- Medical records
- The tattoo number, registry address and phone number
- A written description of the cat

## MAKE SURE HE'S NOT FORGOTTEN

It's a good idea to make provisions for your pets in the event of your death. If a friend or relative doesn't speak up on your cat's behalf, it could be sent to a shelter or even sold to a laboratory. Entrust their care to someone you know and trust.

Since animals are possessions under the law, include provisions for their care in your will. If you don't have a will, write a letter stating how you want your cats to be taken care of.

If you have a medical power of attorney, insert a line about what to do with your pets if you become incapacitated. Give the instructions to your best friend or your lawyer.

# ADOPTION

*The difficulty with marriage is that we fall in love with a personality, but must live with a character.*

—PETER DEVRIES

Adoption is the most fun and the most crucial of all cat decisions. But it's easy to bring a quiet cat home and find out that he is really a talker. Or, to adopt a cat born to jump and be hyperactive when you really wanted one that thought moving from one side of the bed to another was a big trip.

Like people, cats have all kinds of personalities. Each one is unique. Most people cannot live with just any cat. Since each cat is different, it's better to think about the process as a marriage, not an adoption. Although divorce is an option, you want to avoid that with a thorough, unhurried courtship.

The main goal of this chapter is to help you adopt a cat you are happy with, not just a cat who is happy with you. It will help you reduce the chance of bringing home, and keeping, the wrong cat. And if you already have a cat, there is a wealth of general information in this chapter. Read this chapter, even if you are a seasoned cat owner.

## DO I REALLY WANT A CAT?

Before you even head out to look for a new cat, know what you are getting into. Despite their reputation for being aloof, cats are not animals you can ignore. If you aren't prepared to spend time with them, don't get one.

If you have never owned cats, you may not realize that cats do certain cat things, and need certain things. New, unsuspecting cat owners may be surprised when they find their cats regularly:

• Jump. Cats like to be in high places (on top of your

⚠ **WARNING**

**Cats should NOT be given as a surprise birthday or Christmas present!**

Getting the right cat is worth the wait. If it's your child's birthday present, don't settle for one simply because it's her birthday. If the right cat for you and your child isn't available by that day, it's better to wait.

Your child will appreciate being included to help pick out the cat. Pick a day you both can visit a few shelters. Give her an idea of how many different personalities she has to choose from.

desk, bookcase, filing cabinet, sofa) to watch people and events and gain information about people behavior.

- Play. Cats need interaction with humans. Be prepared to spend time playing with and talking to your cat.

- Scratch. Cats have to scratch. Rather than trying to prevent them, train them to use a scratching post and trim their claws regularly.

- Vomit. Enough said.

## CAN I ACCOMMODATE A CAT?

Where you live plays an important role in the feasibility of owning a cat, especially if you don't own your own home. Obviously, some landlords do not allow cats so locate apartments that do. One way is to find someone who has a computer with Internet access. You can do searches on the Internet for apartments that allow cats. When you do find a place you want to live, think about the following.

- Does your apartment complex require declawing or require that cats are kept indoors only? If so, you could face unresolvable litter box problems that could eat up your security deposit and living options.

- Is your apartment or home big enough for one or more scratching posts or litter boxes? Can it handle more litter boxes if a problem develops?

- Are you on a quiet street or a busy boulevard? If you live in a congested area, your cat will face increased risks if he goes outdoors.

## WHERE DO I FIND A GOOD CAT TO ADOPT?

Shelters are unquestionably the best place to find a cat. With thousands of cats being euthanized in your local cat shelters due to lack of homes, adoption is a responsible choice.

Contrary to popular belief, cat shelters don't harbor "rejects." They put cats through adoption tests so your chance of finding a smart, loyal and appreciative cat is extremely high in practically any reputable shelter in the country.

Kittens less than eight weeks old are often cared for in a volunteer foster home until old enough to adopt. In these cases, the shelter may be able to give you an idea of the kitten's personality and behavior.

Try to locate a small, nonprofit cat shelter. Smaller shelters often don't cage or euthanize their cats. Many small shelters are run by people who will sacrifice everything to find homes for the cats they rescue.

## WHAT KIND OF CAT DO I WANT?

At the shelter, you'll encounter strays and unwanted adults and kittens that have been put up for adoption. I've had very good luck with stray cats. Even after the stress of being captured, relocated and caged, I've trained my stray cats to be well-behaved.

If you're thinking of owning only one cat, try to find a cat who is used to being alone. This will probably be an adult. If you want a kitten, it's best to adopt at least two kittens so each will have a friend.

There are advantages to adopting an adult cat. While it's hard to know what sort of cat a kitten will become, you'll know the size and personality of the grown cat in relation to your home or apartment.

If you do adopt kittens, try to get them over 10 to 12 weeks old. The longer a kitten stays with her mother, the better your chances of having a healthy, stress-tolerant cat.

Call different shelters to see if they have older kittens and at what age the kittens were taken from the mother. Find out if the kittens were fostered in a household with children for several weeks. Children and frequent handling make for a social and loving cat.

Be patient. If a shelter doesn't have what you are looking for this week, they will soon, probably within a month or two. Animal rescue teams are likely to encounter any breed, color or temperament you want. They can let you know when the exact cat you are looking for arrives.

## OTHER WAYS TO FIND A CAT

During kitten season (about March to October) and when college semesters end, you can find lots of free cats. Many college students think they want a cat. Later, when they realize they have no place for it during the summer, they surrender it to the shelter or abandon it to fend for itself. Post signs on campus to try to get the cat before he's abandoned.

Newspaper ads are a good resource. And some pet stores allow nonprofit animal rescue shelters to use a section of their store or office to display rescued cats.

Fostering is perhaps the best option of all, because you get to live with the cat for a while. Many shelters have fostering programs. You care for their cats in your home until they are ready for adoption. In essence, you get to try out a lot of cats.

## WHERE *NOT* TO GET A CAT

Avoid pet stores unless the adoptions are sponsored by a nonprofit agency. Conscientious breeders do not sell kittens or puppies to pet stores. Good breeders want to interview adoption candidates to help find good homes for the pets they've nurtured. Few pet stores put out the effort to ensure a good home.

As I said in the beginning of this book, I recommend not getting a feral cat. They are difficult and often impossible to train. Some cat owners spend years getting a feral to accept humans.

## HOW MANY CATS DO I WANT?

Deciding how many cats you can have in your home depends on the space you have available, both indoors and outdoors. It also depends on the amount of time, money, effort and patience you have for taking care of them.

While I cannot predict what the right number of cats is for your situation, I do recommend that you have at least two cats. Cats are social animals by nature. And two cats who get along will groom and play with each other.

## OWNING AN ONLY CAT

If a second cat is out of the question, here are some ways you can help keep your only cat happy.

- Spend as much time as you can playing and being with him. Lure toys, supervised outside walks and daily massages can really help.

- Help groom him. Pet and scratch your cat often in places he can't lick: his head and neck and under his chin. Groom him more often.

- Leave a light and radio on when you're not home.

- Have special bed, just for him.

- Provide distractions while you're gone or busy: bird feeder, TV, aquarium to watch, safe toys to play with.

- Some companies sell VCR videos that are made especially for cats to watch. They have birds and other wildlife sounds. (My cats like to watch these sometimes.)

- See the special section for indoor-only cats in the Outside/Inside chapter. Many only cats are kept indoors only, as well as being alone.

For more suggestions on keeping the only cat happy, read *51 Ways to Entertain Your Housecat While You're Out* by Stephanie Laland.

## SPOTTING A HEALTHY CAT

Cats available for adoption in shelters are usually physically healthy, but you can do your own check for physical and mental health while the cat is still at the shelter.

First, pay attention to these things to see if a cat is interested in being with people:

- When you walk by her cage, does she stand up and try to get your attention?

- Does she stick her paw outside the cage and try to reach for you in a loving way?

If you find one you are interested in, ask the attendant to take the cat out of the cage. As you play with him, observe the following:

- Are his eyes clear, bright and curious, or watery and half-closed? Does he move his head to watch you? If only his eyes follow you, he may be frightened of his current situation. Or he may just be too frightened to trust anyone for now, and mellow out when he gets home.

- Does he notice things? Is he playful? Does he hear the snap of your fingers? Take an interest in you or others? Sniff the air? A cat who takes no interest could be very sick or very frightened.

- How does the cat move and walk? Does he purr when you pet him? Does he rub up against you? Does he put his tail straight up when he walks or runs or when you pet him? These are signs that he is happy to see you.

- Are there any fleas, ticks or ear mites present? Have the shelter help you check for these nasty critters because body parasites can be very difficult to get rid of. While fleas and ticks may take more than one treatment, don't let fleas or ticks prevent you from adopting a cat. (I adopted Sam knowing he had ear mites. I had to treat his ear mites about once every five years and he lived to be over 16 years old. The other cats I had at the time never contracted ear mites.)

- Does he talk (meow) too much for you? It's like getting a barker— some people want noisy pets and some don't. Be forewarned. The cat won't change.

- Is he declawed? My advice is, don't adopt him. Declawed cats usually require more time and money because they are physically challenged. In some cases, the adoption papers of declawed cats carry a statement like, "not suitable for homes with children under the age of four" because they tend to bite more often than clawed cats.

- Is he sleeping in his litter box? Unless the cat is allowed outside, to pee somewhere else, a cat who's sleeping in his toilet could have severe emotional problems.

- How does he act when he walks by other cats? Does he hiss and growl? Hissing at cats or dogs is okay but if a cat shows these signs of aggression against people, I'd think twice about adopting him.

- Is the cat responsive to touch? Does he bite you for easy petting or does it take aggressive petting to get him agitated? You may want to avoid a cat who snaps at you too easily. Some clawed cats can have a nervous bite that will go away after a few weeks in your home, but declawed cats aren't as likely to stop biting.

- Is he affectionate? Gently stroke his stomach and see if he purrs. Cats who let you rub their stomachs usually trust humans.

Once you've found a cat you like, find out what the shelter already knows about the particular cat you're interested in. Look at the adoption papers, which might give you clues as to how the cat will act around other cats, dogs or

**CATS ARE LIKE PEOPLE**

The more fair-skinned we are, the more vulnerable we are to the sun rays.

children. Usually the papers state how or why the cat ended up in the shelter. If you can, talk to the people who fostered the cat to find out more about its personality and habits.

Finally, like people, each cat has an individual personality that must be respected. You can train him to use a scratching post, but if he's a jumper or a talker, you won't change that. Looks are not enough; fall in love with his personality.

## OTHER THINGS TO CONSIDER

### COSTS

A "free" cat is never free of expenses. Before you bring a cat home, make sure you can afford to keep him. Adoption fees range from $25 to $60, which should include altering and first shots. These fees do not cover all the shelter's costs-at any price you're getting a deal while helping your community.

The adoption fee may not include a feline leukemia test, which may cost you about $25 at the vet. If the price of test and adoption is hard to get, you may not be able to afford a cat; his upkeep is much more than these one-time costs. Be aware that you'll also be spending at least $60 a year on cat litter, not to mention the money you'll spend on food, toys, scratching posts, cat beds, shots, etc.

### OUTDOORS VS. INDOORS

If you adopt an adult cat that's used to being outside, and then keep him inside, you both may be in for trouble, or you may not. There are some cats that have lived outside that cannot be kept in. Adaptability to the indoors is dependent on each individual cat. Many adult cats can get used to living inside, just not every one. To be on the safe side, if you're planning to let a cat outdoors, adopt a cat who is used to being outdoors. If it's going to be an indoor-only cat, stick to one who's already used to the indoors or get a young cat or a very old one.

Some shelters don't allow you to adopt if you'll be letting the cat outside. I have met some people who agreed to keep the cat indoors but really planned to let him out. They believed that outside walks are important to good health and behavior or felt that keeping a cat inside is cruel.

## MALE VS. FEMALE

Gender is a personal choice. No trait is guaranteed in either sex-it depends more on each individual cat. However, my husband and I have both found that male cats like being held more than female cats do. And we also notice males have a bit more of a "laid back" attitude. But again, no trait is true for *every* male or female.

Neutered males cats usually won't spray indoors. When neutered early enough, they often won't even spray outdoors because they were fixed before starting the habit.

### COLOR, BREED AND HAIR LENGTH

Siamese are thought of as "talkers" or loners. Of course, not every Siamese is these things. Tortoise, black, white, calico, tabby, orange-all have somewhat different personalities. You need to check out each individual cat. Just because he's cute or "looks neat" doesn't mean he'll make a neat pet. If you adopt based on color, looks or breed alone, you may be sorry.

One drawback of the color white: white cats are more susceptible to sunburn, which can lead to skin cancer or other skin problems. As a result, white cats should not be kept outdoors. You can let them out for a short while if you apply a baby-safe sunscreen to her ears and sparsely haired spots on her face and nose.

Hair length can make a big difference on the amount of clean-up and grooming you have to do. Many people are allergic to cat hair and owning a shorthaired cat can cut down on the severity of these reactions.

## CATS ARE LIKE PEOPLE

The essential core personality of all of us cannot be changed. No matter how many doctors or professionals we hire, we each have our desires that will not budge.

In addition, we can't love every cat or person we meet. We definitely cannot live with every cat or person we meet.

**TRUE STORY**

Black cats are reputed to be unlucky. But in ancient Egypt, and in Great Britain today, people think black cats bring good luck. I do too.

### BLACK MALE CATS

Here I will plug my personal choice: Black male cats are the best. They are the smartest and the most lovable and loyal. What's more, black male cats are not in high demand. Smart ones are extremely easy to find. A few shelters even have reduced adoption fees for black dogs or cats. You are likely to be saving a life since they are often the first to be destroyed.

### A NOTE ABOUT DECLAWED CATS

Cats tend to compensate when playing with other cats that are weak, old or disabled so it's okay to mix clawed cats with declawed cats. As we will explain later, for health and cost considerations, it's best not to adopt a declawed cat. Declawed cats are easily stressed, which makes them more difficult to own and more difficult for them to accept new situations. Any changes in a declawed cat's life can trigger health or litter box problems.

## RETURNING A CAT

The most common adoption mistake is thinking that just because you brought this cat home he should live with you no matter what. Not all cats fit all cat owners.

As the quote at the beginning of this chapter suggests, if you're serious about being a cat owner, marry your cat, don't adopt it. Most people feel compelled to keep the cat because they brought it home. We really should divorce the ones we don't love, can't trust or can't stand. So before adopting from any shelter, find out what the return policy is. Make sure you can return a cat up to six months after adoption as some adult cats take awhile to show their true colors in your home.

Because adoption is often traumatic, it can take cats more than two weeks to adjust. Because the adjustment period for adult cats is longer than for kittens, keep an adult cat for two months before returning him. Even though a shelter may scoff at your returning a cat, remember that it's you, not them, who has to live with the cat.

Foster homes keep cats for as long as three to four months. (One time, I had to keep a foster cat almost 6 months before she was healthy to adopt. She settled into her new home, no problem.) Try not to feel bad about finding another home for an adult cat you've had for a few months.

Kittens are a different story. Try to return a kitten within two weeks if he isn't working out. Kittens have an easier time getting adopted.

If you want to find your cat another home yourself, tell your friends, advertise in the newspaper, and post signs that you have a cat to give away. Ask a potential owner how she feels about feeding, sleeping, declawing and hitting. Will the cat be living outside only? Alone? Set the criteria since you probably know best what this cat likes or needs. If possible, visit the new owner's home. Ask her to return the cat if things don't work out.

**RELATED CHAPTERS AND APPENDICES**
- *Fix 'em Good!*
- *Newcomer*
- *Safety*
- *Lost and Found*
- *Outside/Inside*
- *Aggression*
- *Cat Maintenance Schedule*

# THE NEWCOMER

*By associating with the cat,
one only risks becoming richer.*

—COLETTE

**SHOPPING LIST**

See the indicated chapters for further information on each item.

In this chapter
✓ cat carrier
✓ vitamins

In *Diet*
✓ cat food and catnip
✓ food and water bowls

In *Litter Boxes, Etc.* (appendix)
✓ litter box and litter

In *Cat Beds*
✓ cat bed

In *Scratching Posts, Exercise & Play*
✓ cat toys
✓ scratching post

In *Hair and Nails*
✓ nail trimmers

In *Cat Safety*
✓ bright, breakaway cat collar with bell

In *Yucky Stuff* (optional)
✓ kitty oats

Also get:
✓ radio
✓ night light (sensor night light works great)

Recommended reading
✓ *The New Natural Cat* by Anitra Frazier

Your new cat's first few weeks in your home is a critical time. You'll be laying the groundwork for your new relationship. And remember, "Cats are like people." First impressions are important.

If this is your first cat, get ready for one of life's great pleasures. Cats are great! But they can be problems if you go against their grain. This chapter is intended to get you off on the right foot.

## HOUSEBREAKING AND CONFINEMENT

Housebreaking a cat is different than housebreaking a dog. Dogs need to be trained to go to the "bathroom" (which is outside). From age one month, cats naturally use the litter box. "Housebreaking a cat" (at least in this book) means to teach him to use the scratching post and to develop a bond with people.

Confinement is a necessary part of housebreaking. Use a bathroom if you can. It should be large enough to have the litter box at least four feet or so from a "clean" area for his bed, food, water and scratching post.

If you can't use a bathroom, cover any furniture so the only thing he can scratch is the scratching post. If there's a window, make sure the cat can't get out and it's not leaking cold drafts.

## THE FIRST DAY

Bring the cat home in a carrier. Your new cat may be scared and intimidated by the new situation. Then again, maybe he'll be out happily exploring the house on the first day.

Whatever the case, you don't want to give any cat more than he can handle. To be safe, take him directly to his confinement room or nursery and close the door. It's a good idea to have a wet meal—canned, homemade or cooked food—ready before you let him out of his carrier. (Remember, first impressions are important.)

Have only one person in the room when the cat is first allowed outside the carrier. Another person may overwhelm him, at least during the first hour. When opening the carrier door, speak very gently and encouragingly. Be friendly and sensitive. If he walks towards you, say encouraging words and his name with pride and joy. To help him get acquainted with the surroundings, show him the wet meal and the litter box. If he runs and hides, don't use his name or say much until he's more relaxed.

Keep his first day as positive, gentle and quiet as possible by limiting the number of visitors. If possible, sit with him through wet meals and for a half hour to an hour before leaving him alone in his room. By then he'll probably want to nap. Keep a radio on low volume and provide a night light when it's dark to keep him company.

Until your new cat sees a veterinarian, wash your hands after you pet the new cat and before you handle other pets.

If you have other cats, be sure to give them extra attention during the first month or so of the new arrival, so they don't get jealous.

Place the empty cat carrier in a room where your other cats can check it out. This will acquaint them with the smell of the new cat.

## SPECIAL CONSIDERATIONS FOR KITTENS

Healthy kittens are always hungry. If he skips just one meal, call the veterinarian.

To help him mature, if he'll eat that many, feed him as many as five wet meals a day.

Start handling your kittens as soon as you get them. Gently pick them up and carry them around. Cuddle them, talk to them. All this contact domesticates them.

Kittens need to learn right away that they shouldn't bite or scratch bare skin. Even though it might be cute now, it won't be later. Always use a lure toy or other item for playing, not your hands, even on the first day.

You can let kittens out of the nursery when you can watch them as soon as they are litter box trained. Usually this takes no more than a month. Be careful that other pets do not harm him. Don't let them climb curtains or furniture. For more information, see the section about kittens in the Scratching Post Exercise and Play chapter. Keep using the nursery until he has learned not to scratch the wrong things. This could take until he's six months old.

If he's an only kitten, keep him in your bedroom at night after he's litter box trained. If you are not pregnant, let him sleep in bed with you. To prevent smothering the kitten while you're asleep, consider putting his bed directly on top of your bed.

## THE FIRST WEEK

Take the cat to a veterinarian for a complete physical and immunization. Shelters generally don't do a comprehensive examination. (Also see the Cat Maintenance Schedule in the appendix.)

Once the cat is used to his surroundings, have all the family visit him as much as possible. Wait a few days before introducing other cats or dogs.

To reduce the stress of relocation, include a multivitamin like Tasha's Herbs For Cats (any formula), once a day on a wet meal.

Make sure the cat is eating! If not, call the shelter or a veterinarian right away.

Call him before serving wet foods during confinement. Call him by his name, say, "Here, Louie," for example, even if he's only a foot away. This helps train him to come when called.

Don't let him scratch or bite you even while playing.

Start gently handling his feet as soon as possible. If you've adopted your cat from a shelter, most likely you will be able to handle his feet the first day or second day. Establish good habits right away. Trim his nails as soon as you can.

Your other cats are likely to check out the newcomer through the door. They'll maybe talk, reach under the door, and even hiss some of the time. This is good. They are getting used to each other.

After he's used the litter box for a few days, let him out for an hour or so to sniff the house and leave traces of scent around. Lock up your other cats while he's out the first few times.

Once he's using the scratching post, you can let him out for good. You might want to leave his nursery facilities available for him until he's comfortable in the rest of the house.

## INTRODUCING THE NEW CAT

When the older cat's activities through the door seem more curious and playful than hostile, it's time for them to meet the newcomers. Sometimes they are ready in a day; sometimes, a week. Let all the cats meet on a day when you have some time to be around to supervise them. Open the door and let the new cat walk out of his room on his own so that he feels in control of what's happening.

Keep your voice upbeat throughout their initial meeting. Use each cat's name with pride, as long as they're being good. Don't touch either cat when they first meet. If a fight breaks out, stay away until things calm down. Put the new cat back in his room. (Read the Aggression chapter for detailed advice.)

Have a lure toy ready and start playing with all cats together. This helps relax the atmosphere and make them think "all is normal . . . this is life . . . this is cool." Tell them how great they are for being good.

# FIX 'EM GOOD!

*"In seven years, one cat and her young can produce 420,000 cats . . ."*

—THE HUMANE SOCIETY OF THE UNITED STATES

S paying," "neutering," "fixing" and "altering" are terms used to describe the one medical procedure every cat needs. The procedure involves removing the sexually functioning parts of your cat—female cats are spayed; male cats are neutered.

The reasons for altering are many. Besides the obvious need to control the number of unwanted, stray cats, altering your cat will, in the case of both sexes, make them less territorial and aggressive. Overall, altered cats are better listeners and they also tend to have longer life spans.

Some owners think it's best to let a female go into heat, or to even wait until after she's had her first litter of kittens before having her spayed. This is nothing more than an old wives' tale. Besides, with millions of unwanted cats destroyed every year, and millions more dying from abandonment, there is simply no reason to let your cat bear a litter of kittens.

Some shelters fix kittens as young as two months but I recommend waiting until a kitten is three months or older and weighs at least two pounds.

Adult cats should be fixed before the shelter lets you take him home. Keep your cat inside until he or she is fixed so that they won't contribute to the overpopulation of cats!

## BEFORE THE OPERATION

Call around for prices. In one day I called five different places. The quotes for a spaying operation ranged from $26 to $149.

If your cat eats well, goes to the bathroom normally, and is curious and alert, then he's probably ready to undergo the procedure.

**CHECK LIST**

✓ Ensure litter box habits are okay now. If not, tell vet
✓ Have vet make sure cat is healthy
✓ Ask vet about withholding food before surgery
✓ Take cat in the morning, pick up in the evening
✓ Comfort cat next 48 hours
✓ After surgery, check appetite, keep cat indoors, keep from jumping

**DID YOU KNOW?**

According to the American Humane Association, about 12 million animals are euthanized every year in the United States, most of them because they cannot find a home.

Note your cat's litter box habits. The habits you are observing now should resume within a day after the operation.

Don't sign up for declawing. Some veterinarians recommend declawing the cat "while she is already asleep." The risks and problems associated with declawing cats are discussed in the appendix titled Declawing Drawbacks.

Don't get the cat vaccinated at the same time you get the cat spayed or neutered. It's a lot for that little body to take all at once.

If your cat is pregnant when it is spayed, the veterinarian will abort the kittens. Keep in mind, *no* cat needs to have kittens.

## AFTER THE OPERATION

Unless complications arise, there's no reason to keep the cat at the veterinarian's overnight. Arrange to pick up your cat late in the afternoon, when he's had time to come out of the anesthesia.

When the cat comes home from surgery, put him in a quiet room with a bowl of water, a soft, warm bed, a litter box, gentle music and a night light. He'll probably just sleep the first night, but he might welcome some chicken broth and a little company.

Keep the cat's activities low-key for two or three days after the surgery. Don't entice him into heavy running, jumping or playing. Keep him indoors for one to two weeks after the surgery so the stitches can heal and to lessen the chance of infection in the surgical area. During this period, closely monitor his appetite, temperature, litter box habits and disposition. Any abnormality could be a sign of infection. Consult the veterinarianimmediately if you notice anything unusual. Kittens are especially susceptible to post-operative complications, so monitor their food and fluid intake closely.

Some veterinarians tell owners to discourage their cats from licking their genitals for a few days. I just let them lick.

Your veterinarian also will give you a list of post-operative care instructions.

# CHANGE HAPPENS

*Cats don't like change without their consent.*

—ROGER A. CARAS

Family crises and disruptions affect cats, too. Divorce, death, moves, dogs, new members of the household, or even vacations can take their toll on cats. This chapter offers some advice on lessening the strain on your cats when change happens. All these changes affect your cat's stress levels.

As a general rule, in the midst of any major commotion in the household try to keep your cat on his usual schedule for eating and playing, going outside and other regular activities. Give your cat extra attention when you can. Take him for more outside walks.

If you are really in a bind, enlist family members or friends to help you feed and water him.

## MOVING INTO A NEW HOUSE

Moving is one of the most stressful situations that people and cats ever face. Before you sign any lease, be sure the new residence allows cats and ask what, if any, conditions there are. Make sure that there are no restrictions demanding your cat be declawed or kept indoors.

However, moving to a new environment is also an opportunity to change your cat's habits. Let's say you want to stop letting your cat out at night, now is the time to do it.

On moving day, load your cats up in the carriers or lock them in a bathroom before the movers arrive. Keep your cats confined until the movers have finished loading up their van.

When you get to your new house, have food, a scratching

**SHOPPING LIST**

✓ radio
✓ cat carrier case
✓ bright breakaway cat collar with identification
✓ baby powder
✓ catnip toy
✓ spill-proof water bowl
✓ health certificate and required vaccines for travel on airplane

**RECOMMENDED READING**

✓ *Twisted Whiskers* by Pam Johnson

**HELPFUL HINTS**

To help your cat be more tolerant of change and crisis, follow advice in this book and:

- move furniture around every so often (but don't talk about it to your cats, act like it's no big deal)
- play loud music on occasions
- take him on mini trips in the car in his carrier

 **WARNING**

If you are pregnant, do not handle used cat litter. Call your doctor for advice.

post, a litter box, a night light, water and a bed set up in a bathroom so that your cat can feel at home as soon as he arrives. Keep him in the bathroom until the movers are gone and the home is secure. Then let him into the main part of the house to investigate. Close off extra rooms for now. If you think you need to let the cat adjust to the new house more gradually, set up a confinement room as described in the Newcomer chapter. If he's really freaked out, shut the door to his nursery when you aren't home. Some cats may hide for a day or two and slowly come out when things settle down. If it's a long move, say in a car crossing several states, he may just sleep for a week, confinement or not (like my Sam did).

Don't let your cat outside for the first two weeks or so, he might try to find his way back to his original home. When/if you do take him outside, watch him closely. Try to make new ground rules for this new yard by teaching him to stay within the bounds as described in the Outside/Inside chapter.

Talk with your new neighbors. Tell them you have cats and ask them to call you if they ever cause any problem. Give them permission to shoo your cats out of their yard.

## A NEW BABY IN THE FAMILY

Remember, a pregnant woman should not handle used cat litter. If no one else will do it, pay a neighbor's kid to take care of the litter box.

Ask your husband, children, sister or neighbors to help you look out for the cat, especially while the baby is young. If possible, start the arrangement before the baby is due so that the cat can begin getting used to the change. To get them used to noise, play loud music or put the TV on at a higher than normal volume for about an hour. This can be done, fortunately, when you're leaving for an hour or so. And to get them used to the smell of baby powder, sprinkle it on a doll or stuffed animal once a day.

Keep your cat's claws trimmed and get him trained on the scratching post. Get him used to these habits before the baby arrives.

## A NEW HUMAN MEMBER OF THE HOUSEHOLD

Ask the new person to feed the cat and to say the cat's name often. Be patient. Cats must watch and wait to make sure "who ya gonna trust?" As your new housemate learns more from you about cats, the more the cat will learn to trust him/her.

## A NEW CAT

See the Newcomer chapter.

## A NEW DOG

Be very careful when bringing a dog into a house with cats. Some cats simply cannot stand dogs, others love them. If you're getting a new dog or just having one visit, trim the cat's claws beforehand.

When the dog first enters your home, keep him on the leash and confine your cat to the bathroom. After a few minutes, let the dog outdoors to pee. While the dog is gone, let the cat come into the room and smell the area.

When the dog returns have his leash back on. Do not hold the cat when they meet, you could get hurt. Let the cat be able to get away and jump high on something to get away from the dog. This allows him to sniff the air of the room the dog is in and feel safe to observe the dog's behavior. You can also try putting the cat, or the dog, in a carrier and letting the other sniff through the bars for a few minutes. Then remove the loose animal from the room before releasing the one in the cage. Let him sniff the room.

Keep the first contact as pleasant as possible by saying the dog's and cat's names when things are going well. Unleash the dog when you are pretty sure he won't chase

## CATS ARE LIKE PEOPLE

Change is difficult. . . especially the older we get.

### TRUE STORY

When our Bob and Sam first met they had a tremendous fight. It was so fast and quick that, without thinking, I put my hand between them and was scratched.

A year later, Sam and Bob were the best of friends. They slept, ate and played together eight years until Sam died.

## THINGS TO ASK YOUR POTENTIAL CAT SITTER

✓ Are you bonded and insured?
✓ Can you provide a list of references?
✓ What back-up plans do you have should something happen to you? Or in the event of bad weather?

### TRUE STORY

One time I hired a teenager I knew practically nothing about to care for our cats for a week. When we got home, one of my cats had the collar on under his foreleg and all the ice in the ice maker was gone. Since then, I hire only bonded and insured companies or people I know.

## SAMPLE LIST OF THINGS TO ASK THE CAT SITTER TO TEND TO DAILY

✓ Feed canned food: Lincoln and Louie get 3 tablespoons of canned food; Bob and Marvin get 1 tablespoon
✓ Refill dry food bowls
✓ Put fresh water in water bowl
✓ Say "good boy" when you see any cat use the scratching post
✓ Check carpet for vomit; clean spots
✓ Locate each cat, say his name when you find him
✓ Scoop solids from litter box
✓ Play with cats if time permits. Store lure toys away from cats before leaving the house
✓ Water plants
✓ Get mail
✓ Give cats treats right before leaving

the cat. How long that will take depends on the dog, the cat and the situation.

You might want to make sure that at least one litter box is somewhere the dog can't go. Also, put the cat's food and water bowls out of reach of the dog until they really get used to each other.

## GOING ON VACATION

### TRAVELING WITHOUT YOUR CAT

You need to get away from cats once in awhile or you'll go bonkers. Plan on some vacations without them. Arrange for a cat sitter or reserve a boarding kennel. I recommend finding a cat sitter. Being at home is far less stressful for your cats.

Before you leave, put a collar on your cat occasionally, to get him used to wearing it. When you start your vacation, put the collar on and ask the sitter to check that it stays on your cat while you're gone.

Stock your house with food and litter. Give your sitter a list of your cat's daily schedule for feeding and play times. Tell the sitter never to let the cats go outside while you are gone. Your cat may freak out when you aren't there and hide outside.

Show the sitter where your cats like to sleep, the urine neutralizer, vomit cleaner, vacuum cleaner, water and food bowls, cat toys and cat carrier. Also give the sitter your veterinarian's phone number and a short written description of your cats. If they get lost while you're away, the sitter can provide this information to the animal control people to help them find your cat. Also give your sitter phone numbers where you can be reached.

Tuck your drapery cords away. Store away plastic bags or shopping bags with handles (cats can get tangled in bags). Unplug appliances and tuck the cords away. Prop doors open so that your cat can't get locked in a room or closet. (A cat can accidentally push the door shut on himself while playing.)

Keep a radio on and a secured light, on a timer, while you're gone.

If you have a clawed cat who is not scratching post trained yet and you are really concerned about your furniture, plastic claw covers may be an alternative. They are expensive and may be difficult to fit, but may be an effective temporary solution.

When you get back from your vacation, feed him and spend some time with him before checking your message machine or your mail or even unloading the car.

## TRAVELING WITH YOUR CAT

Most cats would prefer staying home, but if you do have to travel with them, call ahead and make sure your hotel or accommodations allow cats.

If you're traveling by air, you must get a ticket, cat carrier and a health certificate for your cat. Call the airlines to see what else may be required.

Also use your carrier if you're traveling by car. It can help protect your cat in case of an accident and prevent him from distracting you while you drive. Include a catnip toy and towel or blanket.

Don't ever leave him locked up in the car for more than a few minutes. In warm weather, don't leave him in the car at all. It takes less than three minutes for a car to get to 100 degrees on a warm day. A hot car will kill him.

Whatever your mode of travel, bring water and food. Some pet stores sell water bowls that collapse or won't spill. Also carry a small litter box. Put it on the floor for him to use periodically. Then store it in a plastic bag. And make sure your cat wears a collar, including your name and phone number, at all times during the trip.

**HELPFUL HINT**

Avoid shipping cats by airplane if at all possible. It's very stressful and somewhat dangerous if they are put in the cargo area. Cats with short noses, such as Persians, could have troubled breathing in the limited oxygen of cargo areas. If the airline allows it, it's better to keep your cat with you in the passenger section and take a direct flight. A catnip-filled toy or a mild sedative prescribed by your vet may help your cat deal with flying.

**RELATED CHAPTERS**

- *Hair and Nails*
- *Neighbors*
- *Newcomer*
- *Outside/Inside*

# LITTER BOXES ETC.

*With the qualities of cleanliness, discretion, affection, patience, dignity, and courage that cats have, how many of us, I ask you, would be capable of being cats?*

—FERNAND MÉRY

### SHOPPING LIST

✓ Dr. Bronner's Pure-Castille Soap (found in health food stores and grocery stores)
✓ bleach
✓ spray bottle for cleaners
✓ litter scoop/shifter
✓ scrub brush

### OPTIONAL

✓ old large kitchen spoon to spoon out goobs of wet spots in nonclumping litters
✓ open box of baking soda to absorb odors or Odor Eliminator bags of reusable neutralizer (See Products and Resources in the appendix.)
✓ specially made litter mats to catch litter when cat exits box

### ⚠ WARNINGS

If you are pregnant, do not handle used cat litter. Contact your doctor for help.

Also, do NOT put used cat litter in a compost pile. Even though the litter itself is biodegradable, cat waste is not suitable for human compost material.

If you have a septic tank, contact the manufacturer before flushing any litter down your toilet.

This chapter discusses litter, litter boxes, the best locations and what you'll need to maintain your cat's bathroom. (Note, if your cat has a litter box problem, please refer to the Litter Box Blues chapter.)

## LITTER TYPES

Many types of litter are on the market. Most litters are disposable; some are even flushable. Clawed cats are not likely to care what type you use. Declawed cats, on the other hand, are often challenged with litter box issues. Even years after surgery, be could resist changes to his litter box routine.

### *CLAY LITTERS, NONCLUMPING*

Granulated pieces of clay litter are about the size of small-grain rice. One hundred percent clay litters are natural, very inexpensive and available in every grocery store and pet store across the country. They have been on the market since 1945.

Note that clay litters aren't biodegradable or flushable. The clay naturally contains silica dust which is a known carcinogen. The manufacturers say that cat litter doesn't have any more silica dust than sandy beaches. Even so, if your cat has a sensitive health or behavior problem, you may try biodegradable litters. Many are dust-free and flushable, such as alfalfa pellets.

Some clay litters are scented with a deodorizer that absorbs odors or is activated when the litter is pawed at or stirred. Your cat may or may not like the scent so try both kinds.

## CLUMPING CLAY LITTERS

Clumping litter, also known as "scoopable," forms a solid ball when urine penetrates a deep layer of the litter. The urine hardens the litter which can then be scooped out in a hard ball. This litter lasts longer and controls the smell of urine quite well. Some declawed cats may prefer the fine texture and softness of clumping litters.

Because clumping litters control the odor so well, they seem ideal at first, especially if you have more than one cat. But there is a serious problem to some scoopable/clumping litters. For clumping litters to work, they need a "clumping agent." A popular clumping agent in many scoopable brands is sodium bentonite. This agent acts as a cement and may compromise your cat's health. An article in *Tiger Tribe*, a now defunct holistic cat magazine, written by Marina McInnis, details her experiences with clumping litters containing sodium bentonite. After losing four litters of Japanese Bobtail cats, she isolated the cause of death to the sodium bentonite. After changing the litter, she no longer had the problem.

The difficulty can be traced to sodium bentonite's properties. It expands to 15 times its size when wet. When a cat steps in the litter box, some sodium bentonite clings to his paws. Later on, the cat will lick it off. Once it gets into his digestive system, this trace residue will expand. According to McInnis, this results in an impaired immune system, respiratory distress and irritated bowel syndrome. Nonclumping clay litters at least have larger granules that tend to fall off his paws. And they don't contain this type of cement that gives scoopables their "clump."

Since manufacturers do not have to disclose ingredients on the litter's label, call them and ask if the clumping litter contains sodium bentonite. If it does, try another brand. If you really want a litter that is soft and clumps, try SWHEAT, World's Best Cat Litter, and Cobby Cat. They

### ⚠ WARNING

Clumping/scoopable litters containing sodium bentonite may kill kittens. Avoid litters containing sodium bentonite. Especially if your cat is extremely young, has a medical condition or behavior problem, you'll want to make sure the litter isn't contributing to his problems.

### HELPFUL HINTS

Other uses for 100% natural clay litters (nonclumping)

- Garage spills—absorbs oil or grease
- Charcoal grills and BBQs—protects bottom of grill and absorbs grease
- Trash cans—a layer in the bottom reduces odors
- Refrigerator—absorbs odor
- Closets, storage areas and boats—absorbs musty odors and moisture
- Snow and ice—sprinkle on sidewalks and steps for traction
- Facial mud pack—mix unscented natural clay with a little water, smear on face, let dry and rinse off

**JUST A FEW BIODEGRADABLE CAT LITTERS**

Most biodegradable litters are flushable. However, if you have septic tank, contact the manufacture of the litter to see if it's safe.

- CatWorks The Premium Cat Litter: plant-based pellets
- Cobby Cat: clumps, flushable
- Nature's Touch All Natural Cat Box Filler: aspen filler
- Rabbit food pellets (alfalfa pellets sold for rabbit food can be found at feed stores): somewhat clumpable, flushable
- SWHEAT SCOOP Wheat Litter: wheat litter, soft, clumps, flushable
- Word's Best Cat Litter: soft, clumps, flushable

**HELPFUL HINT**

A friend told me that rabbit food can be used as cat litter. It's not only pretty cheap, it clumps a little bit. The clumps can be safely flushed down a toilet.

are flushable and biodegradable. Another sodium bentonite-free clumping litter is Here's the Scoop. Although it is not biodegradable or flushable, its principal ingredient is guar, which is a natural thickening agent.

While biodegradable clumping litters are safe for both cat and plumbing, litter containing ingredients such as calcium bentonite, agar and sodium bentonite may ruin the plumbing in your house. *Some municipalities may fine you if certain clumping litters are found in your pipes or sewer.*

## BIODEGRADABLE LITTERS

"Biodegradable" means that the litter will break down by the action of little bugs eating it at the city dump. Even though clay and newspaper litters are natural, they aren't consumed by bugs.

Biodegradable litters come from plants. These litters are made of alfalfa, corn cob, aspen, citrus peels, pine and wheat. Most are flushable but call the manufacturer to be sure, or if you have a septic tank. New biodegradable litters are hitting the market almost every year. Some litters are finely ground, others are pellet type. Some naturally clump (SWHEAT, World's Best Cat Litter, and Cobby Cat), without sodium bentonite. Most are dust-free.

## NEWSPAPER LITTERS

Litters recycled from newspaper come in pellet form. These are found in grocery stores and pet stores. But newspaper could be toxic to some cats or people because some inks are toxic. Some don't control odor too well.

## LITTER BOXES

Look for litter boxes in hardware stores, pet stores and yard sales. Disinfect and rinse them well before using.

Have at least one box per cat. Add an additional box if they are kept indoors-only or declawed.

The size of the box depends on the cat and his personality.

When adding a new litter box, consider that a cat may not use the new box for a few days. Don't force him into it. Don't put him inside it. Sound positive when he gets near and let him accept it on his own terms.

## COVERED LITTER BOXES

Covered boxes help keep the litter and smell contained, and hidden. Some cats, however, don't like the cover. Covered boxes are generally too small. If you're going to get one, get as large a box as you can.

A covered box might leak unless the top has a locking lid and an inside lip. Scooping out solids is more inconvenient, because you have to deal with these extra parts.

If you get a litter box with a swinging door, be prepared to remove it. You may have to, because some cats like to stick their head out while relieving themselves.

## UNCOVERED LITTER BOXES

Uncovered boxes are easier to maintain. They come in different sizes and shapes. Most litter boxes are rectangular. A few models have a "lip" which is claimed to keep down mess. You can also use plastic utility bins, which are widely available at hardware and discount stores, as litter boxes. If you get them, though, don't use anything taller than a 12" tub (that's too high for cats.) There is also a triangular box made especially for corners which works quite well for smaller areas. These are very easy for cat owners to clean and handle.

## HIGH-TECH BOXES

There are also electronic, self-cleaning litter boxes available that automatically remove the solids. One model even senses the cat entering the litter box. A few minutes after he leaves, a mechanical part rakes across the clumping/scoopable litter recommended for these models, and places the clump in a disposal tray.

While it's convenient, the manufacturers warn that the

motor starts automatically and that hands and clothing should be kept away. As with anything automated, be careful.

In addition, some cats are frightened of automated devices. Just one scare may be enough to stop a cat from using his box. A 30-day guarantee may not be a long enough trial period for your cat. This is a very expensive box that won't be any good if your cat stops using it. But if you do decide to try a box like this, which recommends a clumping litter, try Here's The Scoop Clumping Litter. It does not contain sodium bentonite and forms a real solid clump for a machine such as this to handle.

There is also a box that comes with a reusable gravel-type litter with disposable pads. The smooth, little rocks may be a challenge for finicky cats. Check on the return policy just in case.

## LITTER BOX LOCATIONS

| GOOD LOCATIONS | BAD LOCATIONS |
|---|---|
| Anywhere your cat can see who's coming | Around the corner or behind things |
| Laundry room, bathroom, utility room, basement | Near food, water, scratching posts, beds or play areas. Avoid living rooms, dining rooms, kitchens, bedrooms and areas where the family likes to relax. Avoid garages, places near furnaces and water heaters where carbon monoxide could collect, or where it's not nice to be |
| Every level of the house where the cat spends time | Far remote, dark places; basement-only litter boxes |
| One box per level for sick, declawed, old or very young cats. | One location only or outside only; additionally challenged cats need additional help |
| Quiet places with some privacy; if possible, out of dogs' reach | Where dogs or others may torment or scare the cat while he uses it |
| Lighted and pleasant places; put a night light nearby | Dark and uninviting places |
| On linoleum, tile, or wood floors; or use a nonporous office floor mat or piece of cardboard over your carpet; a surface that is easy to clean | Directly on the carpet-when he reaches outside the box to scratch the litter, he can snag or claw at the carpet |

## LITTER MAINTENANCE

Read the package and follow the manufacturer's recommendations.

With clawed cats, you should be able to get by with scooping solids once a day. For declawed cats, inside-only cats or cats with litter box problems, scoop solids and wet spots more often. Be careful about sudden changes in litter brands, boxes and locations.

Take the poop outside the house as soon as you lift it out because it will stink up your garbage and house. Or, if the litter is biodegradable and flushable, flush it down the toilet.

Clay litter or nonclumping litter usually starts to smell in about a week. Dump, wash and thoroughly rinse the box because cats are very sensitive to household cleaners.

Leave an Odor Eliminator bag or an open box of baking soda near the litter box area to absorb odors.

Wash your hands after handling litter boxes or litter. Again, IF YOU ARE PREGNANT, DO NOT HANDLE USED CAT LITTER. Get someone else to do it.

### MAINTAINING CLAY LITTERS, NONCLUMPING, NONSCOOPABLE

If you use non-clumping clay litters, fill the box from one-half inch to two inches deep with five to 10 pounds of litter. (Some manufacturers recommend levels as deep as three inches but my cats like lesser amounts.)

After lifting the solids, shift and shake the litter box so that one-third to one-half of the litter box is exposed. Many declawed cats, and some clawed cats, prefer stepping on bare plastic rather than on gravel.

To reduce dust clouds, don't pour the litter. Instead, let it *slide* out of bag.

## SWITCHING BRANDS OF LITTER

If you need to change brands of litter, have another box with the new litter. Avoid making a sudden change. You'll need to make sure your cat will use it before switching all litter boxes in the house to the new brand. Try adding a second box with a new litter and see if he'll use it. However, beware, if a cat all of a sudden stops using a litter that he's been using he could be very sick. See the Litter Box Blues chapter for more help.

## HELPFUL HINTS

Wash the box every one to four weeks. In her book, *The New Natural Cat*, Anitra Frazier recommends this formula which has worked well for me:

1 part Dr. Bronner's Pure-Castille Soap

1 part chlorine bleach

19 parts water

Put ingredients in a spray bottle. This solution is good for washing litter boxes as well as washing down kitchen counters to reduce germs being spread.

It's cat urine, not cat poop that eventually overwhelms the litter. By spooning the wet spots out, you can lengthen the life of the litter.

However, if you are lazy like me, and live in a dry climate, stirring the wet spots into the rest of the dry litter will also help keep odors down. This allows the urine to soak into the rest of the litter.

## RELATED CHAPTERS AND APPENDICES
• *Litter Box Blues*
• *Products and Resources*

## MAINTAINING CLAYS LITTERS, CLUMPING, SCOOPABLE

For "clumping" or "scoopable" litters to work properly usually requires maintaining a certain depth. As a result, you add litter as the level of litter drops. Read the package for instructions on how to maintain, and when to empty and wash the box when using clumping litter.

## MAINTAINING BIODEGRADABLE LITTERS

Read the package for instructions. Some biodegradable litters may require more litter up front but they tend to last longer and don't need changing as often-you can simply add more litter after taking solids out. Most are safe to flush. Call the manufacturer to be sure.

## SPECIAL CONSIDERATIONS FOR DECLAWED CATS

When a cat is declawed, a veterinarian will recommend a special litter for a couple weeks after surgery. He will sell you an expensive, dust-free, paper-based, sterile litter made for postoperative care of declawed cats. But just because there is a special litter designed for declawed cats doesn't mean the cat will use it. Some cats stop using a litter box altogether after being declawed.

Once a cat is declawed, he's at higher risk of getting infected paws, requiring more operations. Keep inspecting his toes once a month to check for infection. Again, as mentioned throughout the book, it's best to avoid facing unnecessary litter box challenges by not declawing any cat.

## A WORD ABOUT TOILET TRAINING

Cats can balance enough to use the toilet. It's a great way to reduce litter wastes. If you want to give it a try, *How to Toilet Train Your Cat, 21 Days to a Litter-free Home*, by Paul Kunkel, 1991, describes each step.

# LOST AND FOUND

*Every 30 seconds another pet becomes lost
or stolen or missing in America.*

—TATOO-A-PET

A lost or found cat situation is very stressful. Here are tips to prevent the problem or to help should it happen.

## PREVENTION

Even the most cared-for cat may get lost. These are steps you can take beforehand to make him easier to find.

- Get him a bright, reflective collar with his phone number written on it. Or include a tag. A cat without a collar and phone number is very hard to identify and significantly decreases your chances of finding him. Keep a collar on him even if he's an indoor-only cat.

- Get your cat tattooed. Fifty percent of all tattooed cats reported lost, are recovered. (Dogs have a 99% return rate.) It is a federal offense for a laboratory to accept or test on tattooed animals. For the tatoo registry, see the appendix in Products and Resources.

- Let your neighbors know you own cats. Someone might turn a cat in to the pound if they don't know it belongs to you.

- Take your cat on supervised outdoor walks so he can get to know the area a little better. Train him as described in the Outside/Inside chapter. Should he accidentally be let outside, he'll have a better chance of knowing what to do until someone lets him back in.

- When outside, do not trust a harness to restrain him. Use a cat carrier case if the cat must really be restrained out

**SHOPPING LIST**

✓ poster boards
✓ markers
✓ staple gun, nails
  or tape
✓ flyers

**TRUE STORY**

Sam was lost for five days.
When Sam was about seven years old, we took him on a fishing trip, just a few miles from home. Sam slipped out of his harness (fortunately, I had a collar on him as well.) He was missing for five horribly long days.

Sam was found because we had left a flyer at a building near the last place he was seen. Five days later, we got a call at 7:00 AM—one of the workers had spotted a black cat in the building, wearing the red reflector tag on his collar. When we arrived, I called, "Sam" three times, and he emerged from behind a stack of pallets in the basement.

Sam usually doesn't have much to say, but on that drive home, he talked a lot. He had lost one pound and had a minor cold but was so happy to see me. I got him tattooed soon after this happened and never took him fishing again. He didn't mind.

## TRUE STORY

A pastor at the local church lost his cat. The cat had climbed into a moving van in the neighborhood and accidentally got moved to Florida. The pastor flew there and searched the neighborhood of the family's destination and found his cat!

## CATS ARE LIKE PEOPLE

A lost cat gets confused like a lost child or elderly person does. They miss their homes and family and being fed and don't know how to care for themselves.

## DID YOU KNOW?

Unless they have been taught hunting and survival techniques, cats seldom know how to fend for themselves. Hunting is not instinctive in most domestic cats.

side. A cat can slip out of a harness almost as easily as he can slip from your sight.

- Don't complain to your neighbor if his dog chases your cat and no injury or misfortune results. It's a valuable lesson for him to be on guard while outdoors. Provide a safe place your cat can jump or climb to that a dog cannot reach.

- Keep your cats inside on any holiday where firecrackers are involved. Shelters have a rise in picked-up lost animals during the holidays. A cat can become disoriented by the unusual noise and commotion.

- Keep a picture and description of your cat on hand. Many cats look alike. (I knew one owner who thought she got her cat back. She took the cat to the veterinarian because he was more talkative than when he left. That was when the owner found out that dental work had not been performed on this cat. She was lucky. She not only found the real owners of the new cat, she got her "real" cat back a couple weeks later. Tattooing helps stop this mistake.)

- Make sure your cat is spayed or neutered and feed him right. Well-fed, altered cats stay closer to home.

## HOW TO FIND A LOST CAT

- Act fast. Begin searching as soon as you know your cat is missing. The sooner you canvass the area, the more likely people will remember seeing him.

- Ask children to help. They are often better at spotting stray animals. Describe your cats and leave them your phone number to call if they see anything.

- Fill out a missing-cat report at your local shelters. Visit each shelter regularly and look at impounded strays.

Don't depend on someone on the desk to check—you need to go and see for yourself. Also, visit the shelters in surrounding areas. Just because you lost him in your city doesn't mean he will not be found elsewhere.

- Advertise in the "Lost and Found" section of your local newspapers. Include a description, area and the date he was lost.

- Check the newspaper ads for found cats. Answer those ads who have similar descriptions, even if the sex is wrong.

- Print and post signs in the area you lost him. Make flyers with your cat's picture, phone number, date lost, vicinity and any applicable reward. If lost from your house, post signs throughout the neighborhood as soon as possible so that residents know you are worried. Sometimes someone may find a cat, not turn it in to the shelter yet just to wait to see if anyone cares enough to post a "lost cat" sign. Ask local grocery stores and gas stations to let you display your signs there.

- Sometimes local radio stations will make an announcement about your lost cat if you call them.

- Don't give up. Some cats find their way home after a few days. Some cats will show up even months later.

## WHEN YOU FIND A LOST OR STRAY CAT

When you find a cat, it is very difficult to distinguish if he's a feral (wild) cat, one that's just cruising the neighborhood, or truly lost. Unless the cat has identification, you've been trained with cats, or you've witnessed his entire daily routine, you won't really know. If you really think he's lost:

- Don't touch a strange cat or bring a lost cat home unless it is in obvious and exceptional need. A cat can seriously hurt you. Unless you are trained to handle cats stay away. Contact your local shelter and report the stray.

**TRUE STORY**

Simon was my second black cat and very loyal. When he was nine years old, he disappeared. It was not uncommon for him to leave for two weeks in the dead of the iciest Detroit winters. But one winter he disappeared and showed up on our back porch 13 months later. He walked into the house as if he'd been gone overnight.

My mother and I confirmed it was Simon because of his torn right ear and an ulcer on his left arm. We always wondered where he was all those months. He never said.

• If you do end up with a found cat, call the local shelters to see if they have descriptions of lost cats. Let them know you have a found cat.

• Post flyers and advertise in local newspapers that you found a cat. Include where he was found, what he looks like and how to contact you.

• Read the lost ads for cats matching his description.

• If no one claims the cat either find another home for him or turn him into the local shelter.

# NEIGHBORS

*We all have enough strength to bear the misfortunes of others.*

—FRANCOIS DE LA ROCHEFOUCAULD

Neighbors can be wonderful! We can share common interests in cats. We will help each other when we go on vacation, take care of cats and mail and stuff. But not all encounters with neighbors are positive experiences. Our cats can sometimes cause us to interact with neighbors in ways we'd rather not. Occasionally our cats do something or our neighbors, or their pets, do something that cause conflict.

## KEEPING PEACE IN THE NEIGHBORHOOD

### *YOUR CAT*

- Whenever your cat goes outside, put on a very bright breakaway collar, including your phone number, and a bell. This helps let others know that your cat is not a stray and warns birds as well.

- Feed your cat well. A well fed cat is not likely to roam as much.

- Train your cat to stay in your yard. This is described in the Outside/Inside chapter. Or stop letting him outside or restrict his outdoor access to the daytime only. (The less your cats are out roaming unattended, the less conflict you will cause in the neighborhood. Cats prowl more at twilight when birds and mice come out.)

- Put water and a bird feeder in your back yard to keep your cats inside their own area.

- Get to know your neighbors. Tell them that you own cats and that you don't like your cats going into other people's yards. Give them permission to scare your cats should

### SHOPPING LIST

✓ landscaping netting
✓ pine cones or rocks
✓ ammonia or vinegar
✓ bright, breakaway collar with bell

### OPTIONAL

✓ electronic deterrents
✓ electronic fences
✓ fence guard
✓ outdoor kennel

### TRUE STORY

There was a biscuit factory in England that was losing thousands of dollars worth of food to mice. The owners tried everything—poison, traps, even hunting dogs. But the dogs ate more biscuits than they saved. When all else failed, a dozen cats were brought in. Within a few weeks, all the rats and mice were gone and the factory inventory was saved!

**HELPFUL HINT**

If you or your neighbor have a spot in the yard you would like to protect from cats spraying, such as bushes, try a wide layer of pine cones or decorative rocks.

**TRUE STORY**

My neighbor's big, gray cat comes into our yard everyday. I like him to because he's so big that he's very effective in keeping all other cats away. And he reminds my cats they are not the only cats in the world.

My cats (minus Lincoln) and Gray Baby will lie out on the patio together, in peace. Gray Baby knows not to cause any trouble because any time he does, I shoo him away for a day or two. As long as he's acting civilized, he can visit with my cats anytime.

they come into their yard. Give them your phone number and tell them to feel free to call. Avoid making them afraid of you so that they would rather call the police or animal pound instead.

• If a neighbor complains to you, be sympathetic. Tell him you understand his frustration, apologize and promise to do something about it. Then follow through.

• Praise your cat when he brings home mice, but say nothing about birds. Don't yell at your cat for killing prey since that will only confuse him (he's not bringing you a present . . . he's trying to show *you* how to hunt). Quietly dispose of any prey when he's not looking. Feeding more natural or raw foods may cut down on the amount of prey he brings home.

## THE NEIGHBOR'S CAT

• If a neighbor's cat is hanging around, either tell him to go away each time, or let him hang around as long as he doesn't start trouble. If you let him hang around, give attention to your cat only. This helps let your cat know that the strange cat is not really important in your life and also, he'll have no reason to be jealous. DON'T touch a strange cat or let one inside your house—strange cats often won't leave.

• If a neighbor's cat is coming into your house through the cat door, you may need to surprise or squirt him sometime to scare him out of the house. Close the door when you are not at home to watch. It's best to avoid the use of cat doors because they allow a cat to come and go as he pleases, which can cause more problems. But if you *must* have a cat door, there are special magnetic doors and collars that will only let *your* cat in with *that* collar. Again, be very careful when owning any cat door. If by chance the cat loses the collar, he won't be able to get back in.

• Don't complain to your neighbors about little things such

as their cat coming into your yard. Unless a situation is very serious, complaining often solves nothing and makes matters worse. It's best not to complain about a dog who seldom chases your cats because accidents do happen and occasionally upsetting your cats can make them more respectful of their outdoor privileges.

## DETERRENTS/GUARDS

To deter cats from getting into yards or gardens, try:

- Landscape netting buried below the surface of loose dirt prevents cats from using as a litter box. He'll get a claw caught and won't want to dig there. Pine cones and decorative rocks can also help.

- Don't use mothballs, the fumes can permanently damage cats' kidneys. White onions or orange peels work for a short while. No cat owner has reported to me that store bought spray deterrents/repellents have been effective.

- If your cat is using a child's sandbox as a litter box, cover it when the children are not playing in it. Try putting a litter box outside in your yard.

- Sprinkle ammonia or vinegar in the garbage before putting it out. This may deter cats but probably won't stop dogs or raccoons.

- If there is a special area of a yard all cats must stay out of, there are a few electronic choices on the market. Sonar devices that emit sound waves as a deterrent have mixed results. The Water Scarecrow may be more effective. I haven't tried these but it seems reasonable for the price and concept. It shoots water when motion is detected. Call the Silvo Hardware Company at 1-800-331-1261 for more information. Ask about item CR34. Although I strongly recommended never squirting a cat in the face with water, if a cat is on the verge of being killed by a neighbor for trespassing, this may be a fairly inexpensive alternative.

**TRUE STORY**

A neighbor came to me one day and said he knew that the neighborhood cats were using his flower bed for a litter box. He wanted to warn me that didn't like the smell and was going to call the humane society and have traps set.

I thought about it for a few minutes, and offered to buy him some new dirt. I felt at least one of my cats was probably contributing to his problem.

He decided not to have the traps put out and kindly refused my offer to pay for the dirt. He turned out to be such a nice neighbor.

But I got a cat kennel anyway *and* trained my cats to stay in the yard.

**RELATED CHAPTERS**

• *Outside/Inside*

- Attach a fence guard to your fence. These are often found in the back of cat magazines, but ask your local pet stores and fencing companies too. There are different brands available.

- Electronic fencing, also known as an "invisible" fencing, keeps the pet in the yard by using a wire buried along the perimeter of the property. The cat wears a special device on his collar. Some models, as he approaches the property line, will vibrate then emit a shock. Others just shock. Models may require a special adapter to tone down the severity of shock suitable for a cat.

  Electronic fencing should compliment outside training. It cannot replace it. I recommend, and most manufacturers recommend, that you teach your cat what the yard boundary is first . . . before you begin vibration and shock treatment. It's cruel to just install a shocking device with no warning to the cat. Train him first (see the Outside/Inside chapter).

  A good electronic fence can be very expensive. Don't settle for something cheap or you may not like the results. Call different companies. Ask what kind of guarantee they have, and how safe it is for *cats*.

- Another option is to install a chain link cat kennel. Make it so the cat can access it from the house by way of a cat door. Your cats can't roam but they can still get fresh air. Put in an outdoor cat tree, shelves or dog house if you can. Add a padlock to help keep it secured.

- A dog will usually keep a cat out of its yard. Buy your neighbor one. (Yeah, right!)

# CAT BEDS

*Most beds sleep up to six cats. Ten cats without the owner.*

—STEPHEN BAKER

Dogs run and pant. Cats sleep and scratch. Cats sleep about 16 to 18 hours a day[1], depending on their age, health, physique, and personality. If you are not pregnant, it's okay to have a cat sleep in your bed, and having his own bed has its advantages too. Comfortable, easy-to-clean cat beds in fun locations can help your cat feel secure, help control cat hair and make it easy to know where he is most of the time.

## TYPES OF CAT BEDS

Different cats prefer different types of beds. Some cats prefer wide open flat beds such as a pillow case with a blanket inside, while others prefer a doughnut-shaped bed that provides support while they're curled up.

Before you invest in a cat bed, make sure it's easy to clean. Can it be washed by hand or in a regular machine? Or does it need commercial laundering? Cats prefer clean beds and will stop using one if it's dirty. You'll need to be able to keep it clean easily.

Brand new beds cost anywhere from $10 to $60. You can get nearly new ones at yard sales and a local animal shelter's rummage sales or thrift stores for just a few bucks. Or you can make one.

Because many cats love to sleep on a clean, nicely folded piece of polar fleece, buy a yard or two at the fabric store. (Polar fleece is usually on sale in December and January, but check at other times too.) To keep cat hair down, fold the fab-

**SHOPPING LIST**

Optional stuff— cats will sleep on practically anything, anywhere, any time.

✓ polar fleece fabric or blanket
✓ clean cotton pillow case with folded towel inside
✓ old down coats, clean
✓ cardboard box with old clean blanket

**TRUE STORY**

Noise does not prevent some cats from sleeping. My husband once had a cat that would climb into his rock-and-roll band's bass drum. The cat would sleep inside the pounding drum for hours while the band practiced for their next public appearance.

---

1. *Except for Louie-Louie. He sleeps about 12 hours.*

**DID YOU KNOW?**

A cat's body temperature falls slightly when asleep. Many cats will change napping locations to follow the sun.

**CATS ARE LIKE PEOPLE**

We like clean, warm, safe and dependable beds.

**BAD LOCATIONS FOR CATS TO SLEEP**

- Drafty areas
- Outside, unsupervised
- Close to a litter box
- Garage
- Near furnace or water heater or cars
- Where he may be stepped on

ric several times over so it fits on top of a pillow or inside a box. Every week or so, refold it so that a clean side is exposed. Every few months, throw it into the washing machine. Since it is fast-drying, line dry it rather than putting it into a clothes dryer. During hot months, slip the folded polar fleece into a cotton pillow case for a cooler bed if he likes it.

If your cat quits using a bed he's previously liked, it's probably dirty. Air it out outside for a day in the wind and sun, or wash it in very mild detergent and rinse well. You can also try moving the bed or placing it at a different height, just in case it's in a draft or he wants a change.

You can also make cat beds out of old down-filled coats. Or simply use a cardboard box lined with a clean, old blanket.

## LOCATIONS FOR CAT BEDS

Try different locations and different heights-some cats want to be as high as possible. Keep the cat bed near food, water and scratching posts, but have the litter box farther away from these things.

Sunshine and great views really help. The most popular locations are in front of windows. Not only is this the warmest spot, but gives him a chance to watch for intruders or birds.

Some cats even like to sleep with the racket of a noisy household. Most favor spots where they won't be stepped on. Older cats need beds near or on the floor, away from drafts, and close to necessities.

Sara E. Levine

# Cat Life

# SCRATCHING POSTS, EXERCISE AND PLAY

*He seems the incarnation of everything soft and silky and velvety, without a sharp edge in his composition, a dreamer whose philosophy is sleep and let sleep. . .*

—SAKI

Exercise is as important for cats as it is for people. Although cats sleep a lot, they want to stay in shape for the hunt. Cats pounce, jump, play, chase each other around and scratch. These activities keep their muscles and reflexes tuned for hunting and pouncing, and their psyches relaxed, confident and healthy.

Scratching is very important exercise. It's natural, which means you don't have to teach your cat *to* scratch, only *where* to scratch—on his scratching post, or his scratching tree. A cat tree serves the same function as a scratching post, only it's taller and has one or more platforms the cat can rest on. Except where explicitly distinguished, when I mention posts or trees. . . same thing.

As a cat owner, you *want* him to scratch to strengthen his chest, back, stomach and shoulders. This releases physical and emotional stress a cat will store. Stronger bodies mean more confidence and higher self-esteem, which in turn means fewer behavior problems and lower medical bills. At the same time, as a cat owner, you want to have nice furniture. Scratching post training is the answer.

If you're thinking of declawing to avoid scratching problems, beware! (See the Special Considerations section later in this chapter on Declawed Cats.)

You will not need a squirt bottle. Put even your cleaning squirt bottles away so your cat can't see them. For many years, people have thought you could protect your furniture by squirting cats with water. I can promise you that squirting will NOT

**SHOPPING LIST**

✓ scratching post
✓ cat tree
✓ catnip spray or loose leaves
✓ furniture cover (heavy-duty plastic or table cloth fabric found at fabric stores)
✓ upholstery twist pins (found at hardware or fabric stores)
✓ cat toys (toys stuffed with catnip, Ping-Pong balls, pipe cleaners, etc.)
✓ The Cat Dancer
✓ Da Bird by Go Cat

**OPTIONAL**

✓ cardboard scratching pad
✓ perfume
✓ Sticky Paws For Furniture from Fe-Lines, Inc., 2924 6th Ave., Fort Worth TX 76110; 1-888-697-2873, or try wide plastic shipping tape or double stick tape. Make sure the tape won't damage the furniture before you use it.

**WARNING**

Be careful with your hands around your cat when he is in his tree. He may act a little feisty there, and that's okay. A cat should be allowed to be aggressive on his tree. If you accidentally get scratched while he's on his cat tree, say "Ouch" and walk away. Later, when the cat is away from his tree, inspect to see if his nails need trimming.

yield the results you want. Squirting only stops him from scratching in front of you and to fear squirt bottles, it does not teach him to use his post.

Training your cat to use a post is the absolute easiest task to teach! He will understand within a few days. A cat who has been badly trained, abused or taught incorrectly takes longer but *will learn*. He's very smart and very eager to show

| SCRATCHING POST TYPES | DESCRIPTION/COMMENTS | SOURCE, APPROXIMATE COST |
|---|---|---|
| CAT POSTS | Very effective in working the upper body. Sizes and styles vary; the taller, the better. Some are covered with carpet, others with sisal rope or fabric, bark, etc.<br><br>The 28" sisal-covered Large Katnip Tree from Felix is excellent for enticing cats to scratch. The scratching part is replaceable. | Pet stores, department stores, mail order.<br><br>Call Felix for catalog at 1-206-547-0042 or write 3623 Fremont Ave. N Seattle WA 98103. Post is about $40. |
| CAT TREES | Cat trees are tall scratching posts, usually with pedestals for the cat to rest. The height helps build both upper and lower body. Carpet-covered models shred and can be recovered.<br><br>The Felix Climber extends to the ceiling and is compact for apartments. Replaceable parts. | Pet stores, mail order.<br><br>Good ones cost $100 to $300. Last several years. Yard sales prices range from $1 to $5. The Felix Climber is about $110 (see above) |
| TREE LIMB | Get a long tree limb 4 to 6 inches thick with rough bark. It's effective and inexpensive. Secure it in an upright or slanted position. | Usually free when the city does spring cleanup on trees. |
| OTHERS | Scratch pads are often made out of corrugated cardboard strips. These pads lay loose on the ground and accommodate a cat who feels like scratching the floor. These should compliment cat posts, not replace them. A cat still needs to scratch tall and upright posts. Wall-mountable units with replaceable pads are available too.<br><br>Other pads that move, such as ones hung on door knobs, generally are not used by cats. | Pet stores, mail order. Cardboard scratch pads prices range from $4 to $30. Or make your own.<br><br>(See Appendix) |

off to you just how well he scratches. In about a month he'll refine his new habit. Kittens, once they are old enough to scratch, learn in just a few days.

Scratching on a good post or climbing a tall cat tree is the best exercise a cat can get. It's the easiest way for a cat to exercise indoors.

## SCRATCHING POSTS

Your cat needs a post. Don't expect him to not scratch or to wait to go outside to use a tree. Get a post with a rough surface, like sisal rope, carpet or natural bark. Smooth surfaces don't let a cat lock his claws and pull, he needs something rugged.

Scratching posts must be sturdy and not fall, slide or wiggle while he's using it. The post should also be tall enough— 28 inches or more—to allow your cat to stretch his body full out while standing on his hind legs. It's a good idea to have a few scratching posts and at least one tall cat tree so that no matter where he is in your house, there's a good place to scratch nearby.

Make sure each post is not behind furniture or other obstacles. Two good places are by the door where you come in and the door he uses to go outside. Whenever you see him use the post, praise and reward him at least once a day. To let your cat know the post is his, spray it with catnip. Occasionally, I'll dab my perfume on things that I really want the cat to know are off-limits. Some cats hate perfume.

## SCRATCHING POST TRAINING

If you're training an adult cat, cover vulnerable furniture with heavy plastic or slippery durable fabric such as used for tablecloths. That way, he'll have no alternative but to use the post. And you can avoid reprimands while he's in training. Clean any previously damaged areas to remove scent before covering. Be sure to secure the bottom edge of the protective cover or the cat will reach up under it to scratch.

**HELPFUL HINT**

If your cat has been taught not to scratch, you need to get him to scratch in front of you. To help retrain a cat, use a NEW lure toy on his NEW scratching post. Also, hide the squirt bottles if you were using them.

**BEST TIMES TO DIRECT
YOUR CAT TO HIS POST**

- Early morning, right after he wakes up
- When you get home from work. Many cats love to "show off" when they haven't seen their owners all day.
- Before he wants breakfast, lunch or dinner
- After his nap
- After eating
- Before he wants to go out
- Right before scheduled play time
- After he uses the litter box
- When he's angry, frustrated, happy or proud

If you have too much furniture to cover, consider confining the cat when you can't watch him for two to four weeks. Make him use his post before he's allowed to leave the confinement room for brief periods. At the same time, place as much protection as you can on the roughest sofas you may own. Confinement shouldn't be necessary for more than a few weeks since a cat will do practically anything to be free. Scratching is one of the first things he'll do when he's frustrated.

Kittens learn very quickly if you confine them when you can't watch them. (See the end of this chapter for Special Considerations for Kittens, below. See the Newcomer chapter about confinement.)

To start training, while your cat is watching, move the post to a high-traffic area and scratch the post yourself for a few seconds. It might sound silly, but smile and make eye contact with the cat during this period—many cats take their emotional cues from you. Associate happiness with his post. If he uses it, even if for a split second, praise and pet him lavishly. If he doesn't use it now, just wait. . .

Cats usually scratch after waking up or eating. As soon as he makes a move to scratch, gently direct or carry him to his post. Speak gently and positively whenever he is near the post. Say his name and pet him if he uses it.

A cat likes to scratch when he is frustrated and nervous. Use these moments to redirect the cat's energy to the post. Sound proud and encouraging when he turns his anger to his post. He will forget that he was mad.

You can also make a game out of it. Wiggle a pipe cleaner or toy up the scratching post so that the cat can't help but claw at it. Play with his lure toy on it. As soon as a claw touches the post, say, "Good boy," and pet him. Reinforce this positive association by continuing to play with him on or near the post.

Use food. At feeding time, scratch the post and say "Time

to scratch." Then wait. If he doesn't take the hint, hold him so his arms are extended and he has to grasp the post so he doesn't fall. As soon as one claw becomes caught in the post, praise him and let him go. Reward him with a treat or a wet meal. But taper off the use of food as a reward after the cat has had a few days on the post. Gradually reward him instead with petting, praise and play.

He'll make the connection even faster when he wants to go outside. A cat who is used to going outside will turn to scratching when he doesn't get his way. Keep a post near the door, and before you let him out, make sure he uses the post first. Either wait for him to scratch it or pick him up and make him scratch it by sliding him down his post until a claw catches. After a few days of this, wait for him to scratch the post on his own. Don't let him outside until he does.

Once your cat begins scratching on his own, it's crucial that you continue to praise and/or pet him for using it every day. He'll especially want to show off when you come home from work.

### DON'T SCRATCH THAT!

The final phase is teaching your cat not to scratch the furniture.

Once he's using the post on his own for a month or so, it's time to unveil a piece of furniture. Do it on a day you will be home, such as when you're doing housework. Keep an eye out. If your cat starts to scratch the furniture, immediately say "No" in a firm yet caring manner. Then gently carry him to the post. As soon as he's at the post, say "Time to scratch" in a sweet, gentle tone. Slide his body down the post until his claws engage. As soon as a claw catches in the post, say "Good boy," release him and then pet a second or two.

Recover the piece of furniture when you won't be there and repeat the process one or more times a day. As the cat becomes more dependable in using the post on his own, gradually remove

**TRUE STORY**

Right before I take Louie on his walk, I say, "Here, Louie! Time to go outside!" He runs to the door and waits to have his collar put on. Then I say, "It's time to scratch." He walks over to his post and scratches. If he doesn't scratch, I say, "I can wait longer than you!" And if Louie just pretends to scratch, I say, "What was that? I think you better scratch!" It never fails. He turns to his post because he knows that's what earns him outside walks.

more of the furniture covers. If the cat has a special spot he likes to scratch, cover it with wide shipping tape, or a two-sided sticky tape by Sticky Paws, until you are sure he'll behave.

If he continues to scratch the sofa after a few weeks, reprimand him more sharply as each occurrence happens. Start showing anger in your voice. Try to get your hands on him as soon as he scratches, point him to the sofa and say "No!" again. Then, either carry him to his scratching post or trim a nail while he's in front of the sofa. Either way, as soon as he's near his post or as soon as you have a paw in your hand ready to clip, change to a sweet tone and tell him he's a good boy.

Your cat will learn that the post is the only acceptable place for him to scratch. Once trained, cats seldom make mistakes. Continue to praise him daily and keep his nails trimmed regularly. In the event he does make a mistake, a blunt claw can do little to no damage.

There are other ways to increase his physical activity, too. Sometimes a cat needs motivation to get enough exercise.

## THE GREAT OUTDOORS

To a cat, the outdoors is a one of the best motivators around. Nothing arouses his curiosity or his hunting instincts as much. A few cats don't want to go outside but most cats enjoy it. Consult the Outside/Inside chapter for advice on how to train your cat to stay in the yard.

### OTHER CATS

Cats love to play with each other. They'll run, tug and pull each other, which helps build muscles and confidence. Hang an old sheet over a chair and watch two cats play and dive together. Or give them something as simple as a cardboard box or brown paper bag and watch how they amuse themselves with it.

## LURE TOYS

Playing with your cat provides additional exercise and helps him build trust and confidence in you. The easiest play motivator is a lure toy. A lure toy is a rod with a thick string or wire that dangles from the end. You can buy them, or you can make them at home quickly and cheaply. Buy a three-foot-long quarter-inch wooden dowel or a yardstick from a hardware or crafts store. Or use an old fishing rod. Attach a piece of cord to the end (use tape or tie it on). That's all you need. You can also tie feathers or strips of fabric to the end of the cord.

Lincoln's favorite lure is a Cat Dancer attached to a wire to the end of the rod. This toy has some cardboard strips on the end of a curved springy wire, and is readily available at pet stores, shelters and mail-order catalogs.

Another exceptional toy is Da Bird by Go Cat. The fiberglass rod comes with a lifetime guarantee and is light and easy to hold. The lures are replaceable, and come in mylar stripes as well as feathers. It flutters when moved through the air and almost sounds like a bird flying, which really gets your cat's attention.

All cats can benefit from one or two play times each day. Find a time when you are both in the mood. It's difficult enough to get them to play anytime so avoid times when they really don't feel like it. Popular times for my cats are after breakfast, and before or after dinner.

Some cats will play with other cats around but with some shy cats you need to keep other cats away.

Pique his curiosity by keeping the toy out of reach and mysterious. After he's chased it a few minutes, allow him to grab it. Don't make the toy too easy to catch or he will lose interest.

It's easy to get distracted so it's better not to talk on the phone or watch TV while you're playing with the cats.

**WARNING**

Never use your hands to play with a cat. You could get hurt. Use a toy.

**TRUE STORY**

I try to take the time to play with my cats every day. They really look forward to it. Louie leaps and bounds up the stairs towards the play room to let me know it's time to play! We spend about 20 minutes having fun with their lure toys.

**DO NOT USE THESE TOYS**

- Balls of string or yarn. Cats can swallow and choke on them. Anything with loose string should be stored away when you're not there.
- Toys with decorations glued on. Cut these off before you use them or else the cat could swallow them.
- Toys attached to thin elastic. Cut off the elastic.

**HELPFUL HINT**

Restrict playing with your cat to one room to avoid him annoying you to play in other rooms where you work, cook or eat.

Radios are okay, because the constant chatter or sounds cover up smaller sounds that may distract him from playing. Some cats will think that you are talking to them while you're on the phone.

Tell him how wonderful he is when he catches the lure or does a good jump. Encourage him even if he isn't spectacular, say his name softly, with pride. To help him feel like a proud hunter, allow him to catch the toy often. If he touches it while in flight, let it fall down as if he caught it. Let him spend time with his prize before you whisk it away. Give your cat the advantage, let the lure toy be vulnerable prey.

Pretend you're fishing and "cast" it to various spots in the room. It takes a few casts for cats, just like fish, to take the bait. If casting it doesn't work, whip it around in the air then let it stay still for several seconds. Stop the action every once in a while to give him time to pounce.

Pay attention to what movements your cat likes. Does he like the lure moving high? low? fast, slow? in corners? out in the open? close or far? Try many variations and see what works. Cats get fascinated when you drag the toy around a corner and keep it there just out of sight. Sometimes it takes patience to get a cat to attack the lure. Many aren't willing to start playing until they've understood the lure's movements so don't give up on him too soon.

End the play time when he's lost interest for awhile, not when he's having fun. If you must end the play before he's ready to quit, go and pet, massage and cuddle him a little before leaving. Always put the lure toys away so that he can't get at them when you're not there.

## *OTHER TOYS*

Reflect a spot of sunlight off your watch on the wall or floor. Or use a flashlight. There are also laser light pointers available from pet stores or office supply stores. (Louie's favorite.

He'll chase the beam all over the place and talk to it too.) Be sure never to shine a laser light in his eyes.

Catnip soap bubbles are available from pet stores or catalogs, or squirt some catnip spray into a regular bottle of bubble solution.

Toys stuffed with catnip, Ping-Pong balls, paper bags, fake mice, anything that can be batted around and pounced on can attract your cat. Cut off any elastic chords, strings, tails, glued-on eyes, yarn or anything else he could chew off and swallow.

Spray catnip scent on toys about once a year so he'll be reminded of the things he owns. To maintain the cat's interest in the toys, rotate them through various rooms or hide them for awhile every few months.

## SPECIAL CONSIDERATIONS

### OLDER CATS

It's sometimes difficult to get an older cat interested in lure toys. To make it easier for him to get his exercise, provide a scratching post near his bed. Although most older cats won't wander far from home, monitor them closely when they're outside since they can't protect themselves as well as they once could.

### DECLAWED CATS

A declawed cat is handicapped. He cannot use a scratching post exactly the same way and should not be expected to. Don't train a declawed cat to use a post. He won't be able to grasp or dig into the post and may end up frustrated. And he'll fall off carpeted cat trees more often than clawed cats. He'll need to exercise some other way.

Lure toys and indoor running around can provide some exercise. Just don't expect too much because cats aren't inclined to run. Playing with another cat is good and it's okay if his buddy has claws, other cats recognize handicaps.

Supervise him on outside walks where he can climb chain-link fences or rough-bark trees. But he's very clumsy and vulnerable, so watch him. A declawed cat needs constant adult supervision when outside since he cannot properly defend himself.

If possible, teach him to swim. Teach him in a children's or chemical-free portable pool, a deep bathtub or a shallow lake. Start with very short lessons, holding the cat in place while he moves his arms and legs. Be careful not to get water in his mouth, nose or ears. Keep the experience positive by having his favorite treat and a dry towel waiting for him when he gets out of the pool. Gradually increase the time and his freedom as his tolerance and interest increase.

### KITTENS

Starting a kitten "off from scratch" is very easy. Whenever you want to let him out of his confinement room, take him to the post first. Hold his paws up to it. Once one claw catches, reward immediately by petting. Let him scratch more if he wants to, then carry him out of the confinement room. The sooner you start noticing a kitten actively scratching his post, all on his own, the sooner you can give him access to the rest of the house. Some kittens may understand at as little as five months old.

As long as there are cat posts available and you there to say "Good boy," he'll use them several times a day—until he gets very, very old.

# DIET

*The doctor of the future will give no medicine but will interest his patients in the care of the human frame, in diet, and in the cause and prevention of disease.*

—THOMAS A. EDISON

When clients say their cat won't listen or has a behavior problem, my first question is usually, "What does he eat?" Nutrition directly affects a cat's ability to listen, to behave well, and to be healthy. A healthy diet is part of the long-term solution for any behavior problem.

## DIET AND BEHAVIOR

In 1932, Dr. Francis Pottenger began a 10 year study on cats. It has become well known for what it revealed about the effects of diet on cat behavior even though its purpose was related to dentistry. In the study, cats who were fed only raw food remained healthier and developed fewer behavioral problems than cats that were fed cooked food. And so it is generally believed that a raw food diet is best for your cat, but it is not convenient. Although you can make up big batches and freeze homemade food, it takes time and energy that a lot of us don't have.

Dry food is hard for the kidneys. Many people think that a dry food-only diet leads to kidney problems. Kidney problems are a common cause of death for house cats.

I recommend a combination of wet and dry foods along with some dietary supplements. Feed your cat a variety of brands and flavors to help ensure a more balanced diet. No single food can have everything a cat needs.

Dry food and canned food should have meat as the primary ingredient. Cats are carnivores and must eat meat to stay healthy. Read the label on every can and every bag. Chicken,

**CAT FOOD SHOPPING LIST**

✓ Choose from brands like these: Avo-Cat, Advanced Pet Diets, Felidae, Flint River Ranch, Innova, Lick Your Chops, Matrix, Nature's Recipe, Neura, Old Mother, Hubbard's, Petguard, Precise, Spot's Stew, One Earth, Wysong. (These foods are naturally preserved. The appendix has phone numbers.) Avoid cheap brands.

✓ Anitra's Vita-Mineral Mix, Wysong's F-Biotic food supplement, and other food supplements

**LOOK FOR:**

• Canned cat foods that are labeled "natural"
• Dry foods preserved with vitamin E (tocopherols) or vitamin C (ascorbic acid)

**HOMEMADE FOOD IS GREAT:**

✓ fresh organic meats and vegetables
✓ whole organic grains (e.g., cooked brown rice, quinoa)
✓ Sojourner Farms European-Style Pet Food Mix
✓ food processor
✓ table scraps

*SEE NEXT PAGE FOR A LIST OF SPECIFIC FOODS TO AVOID.*

## FOODS TO AVOID

- Chocolate is poisonous to cats
- Sugar depletes the immune system.
- Artificial sweeteners, MSG
- White flour
- Raw egg white depletes vitamin E
- Canned tuna
- Onion powder can cause anemia. Check baby foods
- Pork can contain parasites
- Milk can cause diarrhea. Raw organic milk is okay
- Hydrogenated fats
- Hot dogs, cake, cookies
- Dog food

## KEEP TO A MINIMUM

- Canned food containing sodium nitrates or nitrites
- Cheap brands
- Artificial preservatives

## WET FOOD SERVINGS?

Give him a trial serving and see how much he eats in five to 10 minutes. If he doesn't finish it, give him less next time. If he eats it all try a little more next time.

## WHEN TO FEED WET MEALS

Feed wet meals around your work schedule. Try to feed at the same times each day so your cats have something to look forward to.

chicken meal, or some other meat should be the first ingredient. Many experts recommend that two of the first four ingredients are meat.

Buy high-quality cat foods. These typically don't have ingredients that may, in the long run, cost more in medical bills. To find high-quality foods, look in pet stores and health food stores. Ingredients in many grocery store discount brands aren't as good. Cheaper brands can contain what is known as "4-D meat": dead, down, dying or diseased meats, which can include cancerous tumors, not to mention dogs and cats, fur, tags and flea collars.

Dog food doesn't have enough protein. Buy cat food.

## WET FOOD

When I refer to wet food I'm talking about canned cat food, homemade food and table scraps. These should be the main part of a cat's diet. As mentioned before, dry food can lead to kidney problems.

Unless instructed otherwise by your veterinarian, feed two to three small wet meals a day. As little as a teaspoon per meal will satisfy some cats. Feed smaller and more frequent meals to kittens, or to cats who are weak, old or nursing babies.

Bring refrigerated food to room temperature before serving because cats don't like cold food. After half an hour, refrigerate leftovers in a glass container to prevent lead from leaching from the can.

Give your cat meat table scraps, home-cooked food, and raw meats and vegetables. Feed a wide variety of canned foods. This helps give him a wide variety of food sources.

It's hard to find canned food without at least some fish ingredient. But avoid canned food that is primarily fish. Too much canned fish in the diet can make your cat lethargic and can even cause illness.

Canned tuna is addictive to cats and will deplete vitamin E. Lack of vitamin E can lead to fatigue and stress, and some cats might start overgrooming. I avoid feeding my cats canned tuna, but I do give them some fresh raw tuna about twice a month for a treat.

Don't buy canned food containing sodium nitrate or sodium nitrite. They are suspected carcinogens. They are often used in cured meats like hot dogs and sausages and in canned pet foods.

## HOMEMADE FOOD

Tasty, homemade food can be a special and healthful treat for your cat. What's more, with homemade foods, you can control the quality. Homemade food is superior to store-bought food.

I know it's hard enough just to have time to cook for your own family. Here are some simple recipes to get you started. (See the Products and Resources appendix for recipe books.)

Chop all cooked meats and raw vegetables as small as peas or use a food processor. The more organic ingredients you can use, the better.

### QUICK DINNER

- 1/2 cup meat (cut up cooked lamb, poultry, rabbit, fish, or raw ground beef)
- 2 Tbs. cooked brown rice, quinoa, or cous cous
- 1 jar of vegetable baby food (peas, broccoli, etc.)

Stir together. Serve at room temperature. Serves 2 to 3 cats.

### LOUIE'S FAVORITE LUNCH

You can substitute ingredients to add variety to this recipe. Broccoli and carrots are good sources of vitamins A, C, D and calcium.

- 2 Tbs. olive oil or butter (not margarine!)
- 1 carrot, finely grated
- 1/2 cup green vegetable, finely grated (broccoli, green

⚠ **WARNING**

Cats with medical conditions or behavior problems may not be suited to eat certain foods. Tailor any of the suggested food, recipes or menus to your cat's condition, and follow the veterinarian's advice.

**CATS ARE LIKE PEOPLE**

People and cats cannot tolerate the same food every day. Eventually, we will have poor manners and poor health, become finicky, and make our kidneys work harder.

pepper, parsley, etc.)
- 1 lb. raw meat (poultry, beef, buffalo, lamb, rabbit or boneless fish)
- 1 can (about 2 cups) chicken broth or bouillon
- 1 cup cooked brown rice, cooked quinoa, or Sojourner Farms European-Style Food Mix (see appendix)
- dash garlic salt or 1/4 tsp. minced garlic (optional)
- 2 tsp. dietary supplement (see Supplements below)

Heat oil or butter over medium-high heat. Brown the meat. For poultry or rabbit, reduce the heat and simmer until done. Add broth and vegetables. Add garlic if desired. Remove from heat, add grain and stir. Serve warm but not hot. Store the rest in the refrigerator or freeze in small portions. Makes 20 quarter-cup servings.

### BEEF JERKY

I included this recipe because it always draws a crowd, or shall I say clowder. (The actual name for a group of cats is "clowder".) You will need a food dehydrator for this.

- 1 lb. very thinly sliced beef
- 1/4 cup soy sauce
- 1 tsp. liquid smoke
- 1 Tbs. 100% pure maple syrup
- 1/2 tsp. dietary supplement (see Supplements, later in this chapter)

Mix liquids together and stir into beef, let set for 15 minutes. Dry in food dehydrator one to two days. Break into small bits when ready to eat. Makes about nine ounces of jerky.

## CAT TREATS

- Raw egg yolk (not raw egg white; hormone-free if possible)
- Steamed spinach, squash or kale with butter
- Baked potato with butter
- Coconut milk

- Plain yogurt
- Cooked turkey, chicken, lamb, roast beef, buffalo or rabbit (hormone-free when possible; cut into small bits and store in freezer in plastic bags)
- Roasted chicken necks (including bone, crumbled into sections)
- Raw ground beef or buffalo (hormone-free when possible)
- 1/2 teaspoon baby food with meat (no onion powder)
- Restaurant leftovers (no sugar)
- Buttered popcorn
- Smoked oysters packed in olive oil
- Avocado
- Cheese, cottage cheese
- Oatmeal with cream
- Pancakes with butter

## DRY FOOD

As mentioned above, a cat's diet should be wet food. If you are feeding some dry food, feed a variety. Do not feed just one brand. Set out three different brands in three different bowls. Buy small bags and when one is empty, open a different brand.

If your cat is sick, overweight, has a litter box problem, or you worry about roaches, keep the dry food bowls covered. Uncover them as unless otherwise instructed by your veterinarian, for about 20 minutes, twice a day, in addition to the wet meals he is getting.

Contrary to popular belief, eating dry food does not alleviate dental problems.

### PRESERVATIVES

Some of the common ingredients used for preserving dry

foods are considered dangerous by some. Look for food preserved with tocopherols (vitamin E) or ascorbic acid (vitamin C), which are natural and nutritious preservatives.

Avoid dry food that contains

- Ethoxyquin. Originally designed as a rubber hardener, pesticide and herbicide, this chemical is suspected of causing liver disease, kidney disease, skin problems, birth defects and vitamin E deficiencies. Pet food makers often use it because it's inexpensive.

- BHA, BHT. These common preservatives are suspected of causing liver and kidney damage, immune deficiencies and behavior problems. In England, BHA and BHT are banned for consumption by children, but are used in both people and pet food in the United States.

- Propyl Gallate. This is another preservative commonly used in the United States but banned in England. It is suspected of causing the same health problems as BHA and BHT.

## RAW FOOD

You may not have time to prepare regular home-prepared raw food meals everyday, but try using them as frequently as possible. They provide nutrients that are missing from cooked foods.

You can find recipes and instructions for raw food meals in *The New Natural Cat* and *Reigning Cats & Dogs*, listed in the appendix.

## FEEDING KITTENS

Wet meals are especially important to kittens. Feed kittens five small wet meals a day, more if you have time. Pay careful attention to the ingredients of all foods since a kitten's small body is ultrasensitive to foods. Specially formulated "kitten" foods are OK, but not required.

## SUPPLEMENTS

Food supplements help replace nutrients that are destroyed by cooking or otherwise not present. F-Biotic by Wysong and Anitra's Vita-Mineral Mix are designed to help bridge the gap between raw and cooked food. These supplements can be added to wet or dry foods. It's also good to periodically switch brands of supplements as well as food, so that your cat benefits from a variety of nutrients.

## FEEDING TIPS

- Create a quiet, peaceful atmosphere. Some cats cannot eat amidst noise and commotion. You might need to serve food away from where your dog eats.

- Establish a schedule for feedings. Developing a routine is as important for cats as it is for people. Knowing when he's to be fed gives your cat a sense of security and belonging.

- You might want to structure cat mealtimes around household meals so that the cat feels included and part of the atmosphere.

- Call your cat with same phrase every mealtime, like "Here, Louie".

- Don't feed a cat when he is whining or begging unless it's really time for him to eat. Wait until your cat is quiet and respectful before placing any food in front of him.

- Don't feed your cat as soon as you get out of bed. Wait until you've showered, made tea and gotten the newspaper. You don't want him waking you up every morning to be fed.

- Use a clean glass, ceramic or stainless steel food bowl that is wide enough for his whiskers. You can use a bamboo bowl for dry food. Don't use aluminum or plastic bowls. Aluminum can get into the food; plastic bowls harbor bacteria and could contribute to what is known as "feline acne."

 **WARNING**

For any finicky eater, make sure the cat is not sick. Many old cats will appear to be finicky eaters, but are really beginning to die. It's not uncommon for the cat to be dead within a week or so after the owner realizes he's not just being finicky.

Call the veterinarian when:
- An old cat misses eating one day
- An adult cat misses two days
- A kitten (after being weaned) misses one meal; kittens are always hungry

**WARNING**

If your cat drinks a lot of water, he could have a serious medical condition. See the veterinarian immediately, get a full exam and have the cat's urine checked. If the cat is older, have his blood checked as well, to make sure his kidneys are functioning properly.

• If your cat vomits after eating or is eating too fast, spread his food out on a plate to slow him down.

## WATER

Cats who regularly eat wet food drink very little water. Cats on raw food diets may only drink once every one or two days.

Set out glass or ceramic bowls of clean water. However, cats can be very sensitive to the chlorine in tap water. Letting the water sit out for 24 hours will let a lot of the chlorine escape. Using filtered or bottled water will reduce the wait.

Change water daily. Be sure to wash the bowls occasionally as dust will collect in the bottom.

It's also a good idea not to let your cat drink out of the toilet bowl. Water in the toilet is not always safe to be drunk. Also, the seat could fall and hurt him.

## CATNIP

Catnip is a herb you can grow indoors or out, or buy from a pet store. Most cats love it. Catnip helps relieve stress and boredom and helps provide some fiber in his diet. Contrary to myth, catnip is not addictive to cats. They won't sell their blood or prostitute themselves to get catnip. You may, however, have a cat who can pull the catnip jar out of a cupboard and open it (like my Moses used to do). Keep catnip leaves in a sealed container in the refrigerator or freezer. This also helps keep it fresh.

Use loose leaves for eating and rolling in; apply catnip spray to toys. Buy only *organic* leaves to avoid harmful herbicides and pesticides.

Treat your cats to catnip once or twice a week. Declawed cats, spraying cats or cats with litter box problems could use more. Put catnip leaves on a piece of heavy fabric or newspaper. Leave it out for half an hour or so. Roll up the fabric and store it away. Next time, add a little fresh catnip to the pile.

Sometimes a cat will become a little feisty when smelling or eating catnip. He's being protective of it so don't touch him or he may play too rough with you while he's feeling like a "real cat." He could get feisty with other cats, but that's okay (that's their job.)

Spray catnip on your cat's toys, beds and scratching posts about once a year to tell him what's his and what isn't.

## EATING PROBLEMS

### CHANGING DIETS

If the cat is older, and you are switching him to a higher-quality diet, make gradual changes over a two-week period. Young, healthy cats can often be abruptly switched to better foods. A cat may experience moodiness when switched from a relatively poor diet to a more healthful one. He may also get diarrhea. If a kitten gets diarrhea, take him to the veterinarian. If an adult has diarrhea more than two days in a row, see the veterinarian. An adult may have occasional bouts and should improve.

### MR. FINICKY

Cats, after eating the same food day after day, may at first refuse to eat anything else. Some cats even will go on a mini-hunger strike to see if you will produce the food he's addicted to. Don't give in! Instead,

- Try sitting down and staying with him while he eats. He might need you to be there with him, especially if he's new in your household.

- To stimulate his appetite, massage or play with him before feeding.

If he doesn't want to eat wet food, try these tips:

- Use a saucer instead of a bowl. Use a clean one every day.

- Move his plate away from the other cats.

- Feed him a bit of food from your finger. Or try a little

**TRUE STORIES**

Marvin is a finicky eater. But I've learned that I can get him to eat the exact same food just rejected, just by moving his plate a foot or two away from where it was.

My cats will eat a particular brand of food I keep in the spare bedroom, yet they won't eat the same brand served in the kitchen.

**RELATED CHAPTERS AND APPENDICES**

• *Growing Old and Saying Good-bye*
• *Products and Resources*

baby food. Gradually change to homemade or canned food.

• Tempt him with home-cooked chicken, lamb, turkey, buffalo or beef as treats.

• Buy small cans. Some cats like their food fresh out the can and won't eat leftovers.

## SPECIAL CONSIDERATIONS

### OBESE OR SENIOR CAT DIETS

The best weight-reduction program for a cat is a high-quality, balanced diet. Foods labeled "less active" or "lite" often make the cat just want to eat more. With premium cat food and homemade food, cats will usually stabilize at a healthy weight.

Limit feeding dry food to no more than once or twice a day. If the advice in this chapter doesn't help, consult the diet books referenced in the appendix.

Senior cats can benefit by eating mostly wet food. Add a little water to each wet meal to help flush his old kidneys. Older cats can get by with less fat than younger cats, but they still need high-quality protein.

# HANDS-ON EXPERIENCE

*If we treated everyone we meet with the same affection we bestow upon our favorite cat, they too, would purr.*

—MARTIN BUXBAUM

Touch is one of the most powerful tools you have to prolong the health and well-being of your cat. Your hands can heal, soothe, teach trust and stimulate appetite. But if you try to handle a cat at the wrong time or in the wrong way, you could get hurt. This chapter talks about how to hold, pet and massage a cat in ways that can benefit both cat and owner.

## HOW TO PICK UP, HOLD AND LET GO OF A CAT

Pay attention to your cat's likes and dislikes. A cat may not like being picked up but doesn't mind being held. Or there may be certain times of each day that he may not like to be touched, yet other times he will. Never handle an angry cat, you could get hurt.

Approach your cat slowly. Let him sniff you. Spend a second or two petting him. Then, very gently and slowly pick him up.

Once he's in your arms speak softly and gently say his name. While he's in your arms, give support to both front and hind quarters. Cradle him so he doesn't feel confined. Usually cats like to stay upright in your arms. A few will lie on their backs.

Let him go when he wants to leave. Be very gentle. Let him down slowly. Never hold a cat against his will. As soon as he shows signs of being fussy, wait until he's calmed for a second or two, then let him go. Don't keep holding on to him until he gets too antsy to hold. If your cat feels that he can get away

**WARNING**

Never handle an angry cat, you could get hurt.

at will, he'll be more comfortable the next time he's held.

Do not hold a cat when he's likely to be suddenly frightened, such as when he's meeting a new cat or dog, walking near an appliance that makes noise, etc. A suddenly frightened cat can accidentally hurt you trying to get away or being overwhelmed with fear.

When you have to pick him up when he doesn't want to, don't call him. Go to him, instead.

## TOUCH TECHNIQUES

Start with short sessions to build up his trust in you. Gradually increase the time you pet or massage him.

### *PETTING*

Cats love being scratched and rubbed under the chin, on the face, on top of the head—places they can't lick themselves. And you can find special places, too, maybe his shoulders or at the base of his tail. Besides scratching and petting with your fingers, try full, open hands with purposeful strokes, like the way mom cats use their tongues to caress their young.

### *MASSAGE*

Massage is a potent relaxant and pain reliever. Massage is basically some serious petting for the whole body. Muscular cats tend to prefer deep massage, while kittens, old or declawed cats usually prefer a light touch.

Place a towel under your cat during the massage because a lot of hair usually comes off in the process. Speak softly and use slow, gentle movements. Explore different parts of a cat's body. Areas that my cats enjoy are their feet, shoulders, stomach, face and thighs.

When you touch a cat's foot he may pull it toward his body. Go with it. Let his foot stay wherever he wants it while you massage it. If he gets a little fussy, move back into an area that he likes.

Give him a chance to appreciate your touch but stop before he gets upset or agitated from excessive handling. He may bite if he's overhandled. It's good to end with success and him being good, not agitated. Some cats may like only 15-second massages and some may want five minutes. (Louie likes three times that.) When it's time to end the massage, stroke him on his head a few times, gently call him a good boy and walk away slowly, as if leaving a baby in a crib for his nap.

## SPECIAL CONSIDERATIONS

Handle kittens as much as possible. Scientific tests have shown that kittens with just 20 minutes of daily handling are more likely to be better companions.

Massage is especially valuable for an only cat who gets no grooming or physical contact from another cat.

Declawed cats get an additional benefit from massage. The muscles in their shoulders and forelegs are likely to be sore from compensating for missing toes.

Daily, very gentle massage for sick or elderly cats can help relieve stress and pain. Holding an infirm cat or laying your hands gently on or under him while using soothing words may be enough.

# HAIR AND NAILS

*There's no need for a piece of sculpture in a home that has a cat.*

—WESLEY BATES

### SHOPPING LIST

✓ brush
✓ comb
✓ shedding blade
✓ towel

### OPTIONAL

✓ chamois cloth
✓ rounded scissors
✓ electric shears

### CATS ARE LIKE PEOPLE

The condition of our coat/skin is a clue to what we're eating or how we are handling stress.

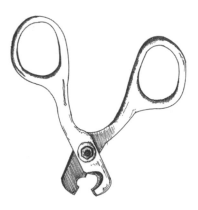

Stainless steel nail trimmers made for cats.

When it comes to grooming, cats are pretty good at taking care of themselves. But because he's living indoors, he needs some help being groomed. Claws need trimming and hair needs brushing. Grooming him once in a while can help keep your home nice and your cat happy. In this chapter, you'll learn how to trim nails and brush your cat without a fuss.

## TRIMMING CLAWS

If your cat accidentally scratches you or snags your shirt, it's time for a trim. Trimming claws is one of the easiest things you can do to a cat. It can be much faster than cutting your own nails.

I recommend nail trimmers made especially for cats. Stainless steel, high-quality models can last many decades.

Before you trim his front claws the first time, work with his front feet without any attempt to trim. Wait until he's in a mood to be touched. Hold him or leave him in his bed while you massage his body, working your way to his feet. Massage his foot. Rub between his toes. Press on the pads of his feet to make the claws extend, then release. If he starts putting up a fuss, let go of his feet but don't give up too easily. Try again the next time you see him napping or relaxing.

After a few days of getting him used to having his feet touched, put the nail trimmer in the palm of your hand before you approach him. Hold his paw in one hand while saying, "Good boy." Gently squeeze the pad of the paw so that the claws extend. Talk sweetly to him just like you do when you massage his feet.

Cut about halfway between the tip of the claw and the "quick" (where pink shows through).

Begin by trimming only one claw a day. Gradually add more claws.

Keep the experience positive by always ending before he gets fussy. Each time, reward him by massaging, petting, playing or taking him on an outside walk. Eventually, you'll only need to tell him how good he is by petting him for a few seconds after his trim.

Once the cat is used to getting trimmed, you'll need to trim all claws about once a month. If you keep trimming a small portion of his claws more often, the quick will recede a little, allowing you to trim farther down.

Be very careful when trimming a claw. Cutting into the quick causes bleeding and is painful. If you hurt your cat while trimming, immediately say you're sorry and comfort him. Quickly trim one more nail then let him go. Play with him to distract him from what just happened. Try again the next day.

Don't trim his nails on or around his post or cat tree. You don't want him to make an association between the two activities.

If the cat growls, stop trimming, say nothing and leave the room immediately. On the next day, cut two, or even just one nail. Leave on a friendly note, before he has a chance to growl.

For hind claws, use the same steps as above. Trim hind claws when your cat is sleeping or sitting quietly on your lap. Trim one or two claws at a one sitting. As he gets used to the process, cut more claws.

Marvin gets his nails trimmed.

**TRUE STORY**

My husband says he wishes his nails were as easy to trim as our four cats.

**TRUE STORY**

After living in a stranger's garage for two months, a longhaired declawed Persian cat was rescued by a local shelter.

The cat's coat was as heavily matted as a tightly woven carpet, and so thick that you couldn't even poke your finger through to her skin. Except for her head, I couldn't even tell she was a cat.

We had to sedate her while two of us used power shears. It took 90 minutes to shave all the mats off. She turned out to be a gorgeous cat.

Declawing typically isn't performed on hind feet, his back claws will need trimming. Declawed cats tend to bite more, and can be more sensitive about being handled than clawed cats. You may need to provide food treats to distract your declawed cat during trimmings or cut a few while he's asleep.

## HAIR

All cats who have hair, shed. And longhaired cats get matted hair. Professional groomers can help you get rid of shedding hair and prevent matting. But I recommend doing as much yourself as you can. It's a good opportunity for quality time between you and your cat and less stressful if someone he knows works on him.

### HOW OFTEN IS GROOMING NEEDED?

A cat's grooming schedule depends on his hair length, the amount of time he spends outside and whether he's an only cat. Some cats may need brushing once a day and some once a month. Cats who go outdoors roll in dirt or on concrete which helps remove loose hair. So they may be able to go longer between grooming sessions.

Shorthaired indoor cats may need to be brushed every one or two weeks. Longhaired cats need to be brushed more frequently.

### GROOMING TOOLS

- Brushes and combs come in a wide variety of bristles, wire and rubber.

- Stainless steel pet combs are good for getting tangles out of long hair. Brushes are nice for a lighter touch.

- Use scissors to cut out clumps of matted hair. Always hold a comb between scissors and skin to prevent accidental cuts. For more safety, use scissors with rounded tips.

- A shedding blade is a hoop-shaped strip of metal with a sawtooth edge and an attached handle. It is especially good for removing fine hair. Use a damp rag to collect the hair the blade picks up.

- Spread a dampened chamois cloth in your open hand and rub it firmly over the cat's coat to remove loose hair. Keep the cat away from drafts until he's dry.

- Some hair can become so matted that a comb and scissors simply won't work. If you brush your cats regularly, you should be able to prevent this. If necessary, you can use electric shears to remove matting close to the skin, but be careful. It's easy to nick him.

- One of the best grooming tools available are your fingers, especially for shorthaired cats. Remove loose hair by roughing up your cat's coat with your fingertips and then stroking it back down. Use a damp cloth to pick up any loose hair.

## GROOMING HOW-TOS

- Find a time when your cat is in a loving mood. Put him on your lap, on his bed, or on a counter with a towel underneath him. Pick a space big enough for him to stretch out.

- Rub him where he likes it to get him in a good mood. If he starts getting in bad mood, stop grooming for the day.

- Start with the neck, chin and head or wherever his favorite places are. If he tries to get up and walk away, gently push him back down and immediately resume grooming. If he gets up again, let him go.

- Start brushing slowly with the grain. Take short strokes, lengthening them as he relaxes. If you use a shedding blade, start with short, slow raking motions with the grain to remove the loose hair. Try pushing some hair so it leans against the grain. Then, starting at the base of that area, rake the hair back to its normal direction with the blade.

- Once you've gained his trust, try a new area of his body that he's willing to let you brush.

**HELPFUL HINTS**

While brushing, inspect your cat's body for abnormalities such as lumps, swelling, or scabs. Report any abnormalities to your veterinarian.

If you have more than one cat, they can groom and play with each other, which helps with both grooming and exercising.

**RELATED CHAPTERS**

- *Hands-On Experience*
- *Yucky Stuff* (hairballs)

- The legs on shorthaired cats shouldn't need much grooming.

- Keep the grooming pleasurable for him. Be gentle and talk to him while you work.

- Stop the grooming session before he becomes agitated or before you brush him bald (which is easy to do if he really likes to be brushed.). Too much grooming can make some cats moody, something you need to avoid. Gently massage him again, tell him what a good boy he is and slowly walk away. Leave him with a positive image about grooming.

## SHAMPOOING

Cat hair has natural oils which shampoo will remove. Regular brushing prevents the need to shampoo a cat. Most cats should not need regular shampooing. I only shampoo a cat if he's really dirty or smelly. This may mean some cats never get shampooed, or as little as two or three times in his entire lifetime. A cat who has body odor all the time may have a serious health problem; see the veterinarian if you have any doubts.

If you do need to shampoo him, be very careful not to get water near his nose. Cats can easily get a cold or upper respiratory infection that way. Shampoo as gently as possible, using very little shampoo. Keep the water on a low, gentle warm flow. A hair dryer startles most cats so towel dry as soon as he's done. Keep him away from all drafts until he's completely dry.

# DOCTOR, DOCTOR!

*Cats are smarter than dogs. You can't get eight cats to pull a
sled through snow.*

—JEFF VALDEZ

Don't gamble with your cat's health. While it is important to treat cat diseases as soon as you recognize the symptoms, it's best to leave the diagnosis and treatment to a veterinarian. This chapter is to help you determine if you have a potentially sick cat. If you have any doubt about your cats health, call the veterinarian immediately.

## A HEALTHY CAT

Somehow cats have gotten the reputation that they hide all the time or are constantly skittish. While most cats will run and hide at the first sign of danger, that's because they are afraid. As soon as they become secure in their surroundings, they have less reason to be scared. Cats really don't run and hide. They are more likely to:

- Play
- Act curious, attentive, alert
- Sniff things, including the air
- Have a good appetite, show interest in food (remember, kittens are always hungry)
- Enjoy being around other cats and people, show interest in family activities
- Use the litter box faithfully
- Groom themselves several times a day
- Walk and jump with balance and coordination
- Scratch the scratching post several times a day
- Seldom show aggression
- Occasionally run and pounce on imaginary things

**SHOPPING LIST**

✓ cat carrier case
✓ towel for carrier
✓ stocking with catnip or lavender
✓ cat treats for carrier case and doctors office

## SIGNS OF ILLNESS

Even healthy cats occasionally get sick. Here are some common symptoms of illness that warrant immediate attention from the veterinarian.

- Urinates outside the litter box
- Has blood in his urine
- Frequently misses meals or exhibits a change in appetite
- Is constantly thirsty
- Shows unprovoked aggression or sudden change in mood
- Acts lethargic or withdrawn
- Has labored or irregular breathing
- Sneezes, wheezes or coughs
- Has white gums
- Has pus around eyes or nose
- Overgrooms or is losing hair
- Stops grooming
- Trembles, shakes or feels feverish
- If a kitten vomits or has diarrhea, or if an adult cat has chronic vomiting or diarrhea
- Frequently cries or whimpers
- Constant body odor
- Has lumps, swelling or open sores
- Obsessively scratches at ears
- Licks around the anus (veterinarian can check to see if anal glands are impacted)
- Walks with his head tilted to one side

## FINDING A GOOD VETERINARIAN

Most people hate going to the doctor. Cats aren't any different. The first step towards making veterinarian visits go well is finding a good doctor.

I recommend veterinarians that will not declaw. Quite often, veterinarians who refuse to declaw are more in tune with and concerned about your cat's needs. This will probably rule out a lot of veterinarians but don't get discouraged.

Ask around or look in the yellow pages for veterinarians who describe themselves as "alternative," "holistic" or "old-fashioned." When you call, ask about their position on declawing. See if they are knowledgeable about natural or home remedies, not just antibiotics, antidepressants, tranquilizers or steroids.

Also ask what they charge. Prices for the same procedures can vary by more than 100 percent.

When you call a veterinarian you're considering, see how patient and receptive he or she is to your concerns. If the people in the office seem uninterested or authoritarian, find another veterinarian.

## VETERINARIAN TRIP TIPS

- Leave a cat carrier open and accessible in the house to help your cat get used to it being around. Put a towel or pillow in it. This way, your cat will associate the carrier more with taking a nap than a trip to the doctor.

- If you're going to a 24-hour emergency clinic, call first so they can be prepared.

- Make a list of symptoms you've noticed and questions to ask the veterinarian. Include questions about recommended medications, as well as their cost and potential side effects.

- To make the trip more relaxing, put a stocking filled with dried catnip or dried lavender into his carrier case.

- If he resists, put him in the case, hind end first, as quickly as possible. If he walks into the carrier by himself, praise him for being so good.

- Give him a food treat every time he enters the carrier whether you had to help or not.

- If you are crunched for time and he's refusing to go into the carrier, put a towel over him and shove him (gently!)

into the case, leaving the towel with him. As soon as he's in and the door is shut, say, "good boy!" and give him a treat.

- Some veterinarians make house calls. If you have a number of cats, see if your veterinarian will make a house call. The time and hassle you save can make up for a few more dollars to have the doctor make the trip.

## AT THE DOCTOR'S OFFICE

Once you've been taken to the exam room, let your cat out of his carrier to explore the room. Talk to him sweetly, pet him and play with him. Give him a treat.

Stay with your cat unless the veterinarian strictly forbids your presence. It makes your cat feel safer and it also helps you have an understanding of what the veterinarian is doing for your cat.

Tell the veterinarian concerns you might have about the cat's eating, drinking and litter box habits. Also mention if your cat is having trouble walking, breathing or has stopped grooming himself.

While your cat is being examined, talk to him and comfort him. Tell him he's being good. In the meantime, watch as the veterinarian checks the cat's ear for ear mites, his teeth for decay and his respiratory and heart rhythms.

Don't allow the use of an injected anesthesia for routine procedures like ear or teeth cleanings or drawing blood. If sedation is really necessary, ask your veterinarian for safer alternatives.

Whenever a medication or operation is recommended, ask why it is necessary, what the potential side effects or complications could be and what your other options are. Because the cost of long-term treatment or illness can become a burden, don't be ashamed to ask about the price of these treatments.

Ask the doctor not to hold him by the scruff of his neck unless absolutely necessary. If you're not happy with how your cat is treated or handled, look for another veterinarian.

If you have a choice, bring your cat home after treatment instead of letting him stay overnight. Being away from home is stressful on cats.

When your cat is back in his carrier, give him another treat and praise him.

Most cats don't fight the doctor. If your cat becomes a nightmare at the vet's, it could be that the veterinarian isn't the right one for that cat.

If your veterinarian recommends an expensive or drastic procedure, shop around for a second opinion.

## WHEN YOU GET HOME

Doctor visits will usually wear your cat out for the rest of the day, especially if he gets vaccines. Don't expect him to be too chipper. Allow him outside for a short walk unless his condition prohibits that. Fix a wet meal when he comes in the house. He'll be tired and want to come in soon for a very long nap.

Handle your cat gently for the first 24 hours after any shot. If he shows signs of pain or fever after a shot, call the veterinarian immediately.

# ADMINISTERING TREATMENTS

*The cat has too much spirit to have no heart.*

—ERNEST MENAULT

**HAVE READY**

✓ special food treats or a wet meal for afterward
✓ towel or blanket for under your cat
✓ KY jelly, Vaseline or oil for thermometer
✓ flexible digital thermometer
✓ cotton swabs for ear cleaning
✓ butter or oil for pill
✓ alcohol to clean thermometer
✓ and don't forget the medicine!

There's no reason to struggle after the veterinarian sends you home with some unpleasant instructions and medication for your cat. In this chapter I'll give you tips to help you deal with giving pills, applying eye ointments, cleaning ears, and taking his temperature.

## TREATMENT TIPS

• The best time to give treatments is when your cat is tired or hungry, as they tend to be least resistant.

• Have the medicine and a special treat ready in your pocket, and all the supplies (pills, swabs, drops, etc.) ready at hand, before you get your cat and start treatment.

• Never sound or act angry. While you're giving the cat his treatment, talk softly to him. And handle him firmly enough for him to know you mean business, but gently and compassionate enough for him to trust you.

• If he resists, comfort him with petting or distract him with a toy and then try again. If you still don't succeed, wait until he's been still for a second or two and then let him go. Try again in a few minutes.

• After any treatment, give him praise and a treat. Try to make him forget the awful injustices done to his body!

• Pet him and pay attention to him several times a day other than just when giving him his treatment. Don't let him think that every time you approach him it's to give him medicine.

## PILLS

If the doctor says your cat's pills can be crushed and given with food, you're in luck. Simply mash the pill into little bits and stir into a bit of wet food.

If the pill must go down whole, coat it with butter or oil. Hide it in your hand. Approach the cat gently while he's still in bed and sleepy. Hold the pill between the thumb and forefinger. Pry his mouth open and quickly drop the pill as far back on his tongue as you can. If it sticks on his tongue, use a pencil to knock the pill to the back of his throat. Close his mouth, this forces him to swallow it.

If the pill pops out, pick it up right away and try again. Don't hesitate, or he will start to squirm and fight. As soon as the event is over, distract him with the usual praise, petting and treats.

## EYE OINTMENTS

It's easiest if you start while your cat is sleeping. After washing your hands, gently hold her head. With the ointment in your right hand, pull the upper lid up with your left thumb and pull the lower lid down with the little finger of your right hand. Slowly squeeze the recommended dosage along the inside of the lower lid. Let her blink and spread the ointment along her eyelids. Then offer endless praise.

## CLEANING EARS

If your cat has ear mites, your veterinarian will give you a solution to clean his ears with. This will take a couple of treatments per day during which your cat must be still for longer than most cats are comfortable with.

Because drops fling out when a cat shakes his head, I usually clean ears in the bathroom. Before you begin, have a towel for your cat to sit on, cotton swabs, the ear medication and some treats. Bring the cat into the bathroom and shut the door.

### TRUE STORY

Sam was my beloved cat for more than 14 years. For many of those years, I believed the only way anyone could clean a cat's ears was to wrap him in a blanket.

Eventually, I realized that Sam wasn't struggling with me because he was getting his ears cleaned, he struggled with me because I was wrapping him up. When I started just holding his ear while I talked to him, the cleaning would last long enough to get the job done. . . on both ears.

Clean his ears as recommended by the veterinarian, usually by putting a few drops of ointment into his ear, massaging with your finger and then swabbing the excess out with cotton swabs. Be very careful not to insert the swab too far into his ear canal.

He'll instinctively try to scratch his ears. You can go ahead and let him do that while you continue to clean. Just be careful to stay away from his claws.

If he starts to squirm, stop for a second or two and start again. Cleaning really dirty ears can take quite a while so you might plan on cleaning just one ear at a time. And if he starts to struggle too much, you can quit for now and continue later. His ears are done when the swab comes out clean.

## TAKING HIS TEMPERATURE

A cat's temperature is taken using a thermometer in his rectum. Flexible, digital thermometers provide a fast and accurate reading. They even beep to let you know they're done. Conventional mercury thermometers do not bend and require about five minutes of insertion before reading.

Apply a bit of Vaseline, KY jelly or massage oil to the thermometer before insertion. Say he's being good while you massage his body and work your way toward his hip area. Gently insert the thermometer. Stroke him and say his name as long as he isn't resisting. If he starts to struggle, hold him firmly and speak in a tone that makes him understand that he's not going anywhere until you're done.

Swab the thermometer with rubbing alcohol afterwards. Whatever type of thermometer you use, write "Cat Use Only" and restrict its use accordingly.

# YUCKY STUFF

*The cat is utterly sincere.*

—FERNAND MÉRY

Sooner or later, everybody's cat produces some form of yucky stuff: vomit, hairballs, diarrhea, and poop. The way I see it, learning how to deal with these vile substances is just part of the job.

## VOMIT

Cats often give warning signs that they are about to vomit, whether it's food or hairballs. Some cats will "yowl" once or twice shortly before throwing up. Sometimes they'll run around the house very fast while drooling and smacking their tongue on their lips. Or they'll begin to dry heave and convulse, a sure sign that vomit will soon appear. If you notice any of these, immediately put a newspaper under him or move him to a noncarpeted area before he does the deed. But you have to move fast. I rarely get to my cats in time so I keep carpet cleaners and sponges on hand.

Cats often vomit after eating too much too fast or eating something that doesn't agree with them. Or because there is a medical problem such as FUS (feline urologic syndrome) or poisoning.

Medical problems and poisoning are best left for the veterinarian to treat. So if your cat vomits after he eats a certain brand or variety, change to something different or try lesser amounts of it.

He may also have trouble with certain kinds of meat. If, for example, he's been upchucking beef, try a different meat like lamb or chicken. Or try raw or homemade food.

**SHOPPING LIST**

- ✓ urine neutralizer
- ✓ mild detergent
- ✓ carpet cleaner
- ✓ rags, sponges or paper towel
- ✓ hairball remedy
- ✓ dietary fiber

**OPTIONAL**

- ✓ brown rice
- ✓ minced garlic
- ✓ chicken broth
- ✓ cottage cheese
- ✓ ascorbic acid crystals (vitamin C)
- ✓ "kitty oats" or "kitty grass" seeds

**HELPFUL HINT**

When my cats eat grass outside, I wait until they throw up out there before letting them back in the house.

**WARNING**

Don't let him in the yard if weed killer was recently applied.

If you think your cat is eating too fast, feed him smaller servings more frequently. Also, help slow him down by spreading his regular serving on a larger plate.

## HAIRBALLS

Cats ingest loose hair as they groom themselves. The hair collects in the stomach and must occasionally be coughed up or excreted in his poop. Sometimes hair gets stuck in his throat which can lead to a dry cough.

Hairballs are the same size and shape as poop. It's easy for a cat owner to mistake the two. Hairballs, however, have a different texture and color. If you were try to "separate" the "stool," it wouldn't separate. It would stay clumped together, and sticky, just as human stools do.

While hairballs are yucky, they serve a useful function. If the hair builds up for too long in the cat's stomach, he may not be able to cough it up or pass it through. This can result in a very, very sick cat. Your cat needs help to pass his hair.

Here are ways to help your cat get rid of ingested hair:

- A hairball remedy will make it easier for your cat to pass his hair in his stool. Hairball remedies can be found in pet stores, mail order catalogs and veterinarian offices. Many cats will lick the gooey substance directly from the tube or container. If not, rub some on his leg for him to lick off. Use a small glob or he'll shake the excess off and get stuff on your walls. Or rub it in with the nozzle of the applicator. Buy hairball remedies that don't contain sugar or benzoate of soda, which is a preservative.

- Half a teaspoon of butter once or twice a week can also help him pass the hair in his stool. Rub it on his paws or let him lick it out of a bowl.

- Add fiber in powder or tablets to his diet. Fiber supplements are available at pet stores, health food stores or through mail order. Follow the directions on the package.

- For additional fiber, grow "kitty oats" or "kitty grass" indoors. Cats will nibble on the young shoots. Catnip is another source of fiber.

- If he's coughing, try rubbing his neck and shoulders, it seems to help.

- Take him outdoors. Eating grass in the yard will help your cat throw up the hair—and grass will go with it. Keep your cat away from lawns that have weed killers until the manufacturer says it's okay.

## DIARRHEA

Cat diarrhea looks like melted chocolate and smells really bad. If your cat has a diarrhea problem, pay attention to what he's eating. Milk is a common culprit. Remove suspected food from his diet, and vary the diet so that he doesn't have more of any one particular food than he can handle.

There are also certain foods that can improve the consistency of your cat's stools. Try giving him:

- Homemade meals
- Organic catnip
- Minced garlic
- Cooked brown rice or brown rice cereal
- Cheese or cottage cheese
- Blueberries
- Chicken broth with a pinch of ascorbic acid (vitamin C)
- Dietary fiber for hairballs, which can also help prevent diarrhea

If your cat continues to have diarrhea problems, call the veterinarian.

## POOP

Cats shouldn't poop outside the litter box. If you think your cat is pooping outside the litter box, look again. The little gifts could be coughed-up hairballs. They resemble each other, so look carefully.

**⚠ WARNING**

Call the veterinarian immediately if your kitten has diarrhea. Diarrhea causes dehydration which can quickly kill a kitten. If an adult has diarrhea for more than two days, call the veterinarian.

When you've determined he's really poopin' outside of the litter box; consider the following.

- He may be constipated. Add more moisture and fiber to his diet with homemade meals, table scraps and canned food. For additional fiber, include catnip and kitty oats. Provide at least two wet meals each day to help keep his "internals" moist. If the problem continues, stop feeding dry food altogether. Laxative-based hairball remedies can also help relieve constipation.

- Switch to a litter that doesn't contain sodium bentonite as a clumping agent. If ingested, it can contribute to constipation problems.

- Clean the litter box. It may be too dirty. Cats are tidy creatures. Some will poop outside, yet near, the box if it is too dirty.

Sara E. Levine

# Cat Behavior

# BASIC TRAINING

*If a cat does something we call it instinct; if we do the same thing for the same reason, we call it intelligence.*

—WILL CUPPY

No matter where Louie is—even if he's asleep, hiding or outside—he comes running when he hears me call "Here, Louie!" It's because I put my cats through "basic training." And it is very easy. I don't use squirt bottles or clickers. I simply talk to my cats and tell them, and sometimes ask them, what I want. And they do it.

Cats *will* listen. They *will* come when called. They'll even learn tricks and hand signals if you want. Although white cats are often deaf, most cats aren't hard of hearing.

Basic training builds strong and useful communication links between you and your cat. In this chapter, you'll understand the three fundamental rules of basic training:

1. Never hit him. Trust is necessary for training. Hitting will not teach a cat to trust you.

2. Be aware how to talk to him. Only say his name when he's good. Never use his name with "No."

3. *Always* make it a pleasure for him to come to you or to come home. No matter what.

Also, throughout the book, I give suggestions on how to reward and reprimand certain good or bad behavior, such as scratching post training and aggression.

## REWARDS

Rewards are a necessary part of training. Reprimands only teach a cat what *not* to do. Rewards should be reserved to reinforce good behavior[1]. When the cat does something good, he

**SHOPPING LIST**

✓ cat toys
✓ cat brush
✓ catnip
✓ food treats

**OPTIONAL**

✓ can of pennies

**CATS ARE LIKE PEOPLE**

We appreciate sincerity. Hearing a sincere "Hello" or "I'm sorry" can make a big difference in our attitude.

**HELPFUL HINTS**

Say "Hello, Louie!" when he enters the room.

Say "I'm sorry, Louie," when it is your fault that he ran into you.

---

1. *Sometimes a cat owner does not know she is rewarding bad behavior. A popular example is when a cat is mean to another cat, the bully often gets attention when it's the victim who should be getting it all.*

### TRUE STORY

When Bob walks into the room and I say, "Hey, Bob! How are you doing, Bob?" his tail goes up immediately.

### REWARDS FOR GOOD BEHAVIOR

• food treat
• a trip outside
• playtime with you
• catnip
• petting
• praise (say his name!)

### WARNING

! Never reprimand a cat for peeing outside his box. That is like punishing a child for bedwetting. See the Litter Box Blues chapter.

### HELPFUL HINTS

Get him more used to doing things that you ask of him. When you think he's in the mood to do what you want, ask him if that's what he'll do, such as "Time to scratch" or "Here, Louie!" The more choices he thinks he's allowed to make, the more he'll make the ones you want when you want him to.

Sound happy to see him. Saying "Hey Louie, where you been man?" can make him feel special.

needs to be recognized. Any attention or recognition to him is a reward.

Rewards can be any thing the cat likes. It can be a "great" reward like food and going outside to something as little and as a short as a pet or kind word. Playing with a lure toy, massage or brushing may also be favorite rewards.

Another reward is simply to say your cat's name anytime he's good. You want to always have him know that when he hears his name, he is good. Cut down on his guesswork. "Mommy said my name, I MUST be doing good or she wouldn't have said it!" This also means not to use his name as an "I'm warning you." And not to say his name when he's being a jerk.

Rule number three says to always make it a pleasure for your cat to come to you or home. This means if your cat ever walks to you, don't do something he thinks is bad like giving him a pill, taking him indoors or trimming a nail. If you must do something bad to your cat, go to him. And let your cat know he's welcomed home. Even if he was gone for several hours, even if he got in a cat fight outside, as soon as he's in the house, he deserves a treat.

## FOOD TREATS AS REWARDS

Food treats are listed in the Diet chapter. Reserve food treats for when he's been through something difficult. Besides making him feel better, this helps prevent stress-related behavior problems. I also use his daily wet meal to reinforce the "Here, Louie" command, which is using his daily "treat" for coming when called.

Unless he's really super old, it's best not to give food treats for no rhyme or reason. Indiscriminate treats can start nasty habits, like nagging and bugging you for little tidbits, throughout the day.

## GOOD TIMES TO GIVE A FOOD TREAT

• When he gets into his carrier for a trip to the veterinarian, while at the veterinarians, and for the trip home

- After cleaning his ears or giving him medicine or other home treatments
- Coming when called under stress
- Always when he comes home! (Or plan his wet meal for the end of his walk)
- To a senior citizen cat daily, just because he's old

## REPRIMANDS

A loud, simple "No" is about the only reprimand you'll need to use. Just say "No!" Do NOT say his name when you use the word "no." But even "no" must be used with caution: use only as much force in the word "no" as the cat can handle. Some cats get offended easily.

Say "No" quickly in response to walking on the counter, jumping on the stove, or scratching the sofa[2]. If he still doesn't stop, say "No" again and loudly clap twice. Keep at him until he stops—even if you have to push him off the stove or counter or pick him up and carry him to his scratching post. He needs to know you mean business.

As soon as your cat stops doing the misbehavior, tell him he's a good boy. Whenever a cat is *not* doing something bad, he is good—it does not matter if he was bad just bad five seconds ago. If he's good right this very second, he needs to hear "good boy!"

Do not feed a cat or let him outside after *seriously* poor behavior, such as spraying or urinating. It's okay to say he's a good boy a few minutes later, just don't feed him special food in the next half hour. And do not put him outside in response to his soiling the house. A cat will learn to do those things to be let outside.

If he stops misbehaving before you can say "no," don't say it. It's too late. In fact, depending on the situation and the

2. *Don't start reprimanding for scratching the sofa until positive use of the scratching post has been ingrained for a few weeks. Also, NEVER reprimand a cat who urinates outside the litter box.*

type of misbehavior, you could actually praise him for stopping. For example, if he starts to jump on the counter and you look his way and he refrains, praise him.

It's very important to consistently respond to bad behavior. If you don't want him on the counter, you need to say "no" *every* time you see it happen. Sometimes, cats will intentionally break rules just to see if you will be lazy today. Don't let it go "just this once" or he will try longer and harder tomorrow. Once your cat learns that "no" means "no," he will often learn something is off-limits by being told just a few times.

Scaring the cat can also be a reprimand. If your cat continues to jump the fence or onto the counter, set up a situation where you can catch him at it without being seen. When he does it, scare him by throwing a can of pennies from hiding or making a loud noise. He is more likely to stop this behavior if he thinks he can't get away with it even when you're not there.

Reserve the word "no" to mean never. When he wants something that he can't have right now, say, "Not now" or something like that. He's not being bad, he may just be whining. If you tell him "not now"—mean it. Do not give in until well after the cat has forgotten what he had wanted.

Sometimes ignoring the cat can act as a reprimand. When a cat is acting like a bully or foolish, give attention to the cats who *are* behaving well. Don't even look him in the eye until he's acting more civilized.

## SCRUFFING

Scruffing is when a person controls a cat by grabbing and holding the loose skin at the base of his neck. Mother cats scruff their kittens to carry them, but being scruffed is humiliating and frightening to an adult cat.

Only scruff your cat when there is danger of injury to you

or someone else, or to himself. While he's being scruffed, support his hind end with the other hand. Limit the scruff hold to as little time as possible, releasing the grip as soon as the danger has passed. I mention scruffing as a last resort reprimand if the cat crosses the street in the Outside/Inside chapter. That will be the only time in this book that scruffing is used as a reprimand. It's also suggested that if you have to do it more than twice, that the outside training is not worth continuing. Scruffing needs to be reserved for emergency stuff.

## DON'T HIT HIM OR SQUIRT HIM

*Do not hit, spank or otherwise hurt your cat as a way to deter bad behavior.* Hitting only teaches your cat to fear you and run away from you. Hitting does not teach a cat what is expected of him and does not encourage him to trust people or their hands.

Getting sprayed with water is a traumatic experience for a cat. Only use a spray bottle or squirt gun to break up a serious cat fight. Keep a spray bottle or squirt gun on your back porch, or where a serious confrontation is likely to occur.

## TRAINING YOUR CAT TO COME WHEN CALLED

It's really nice to have your cat come when you want him to. And it helps to make other training much easier.

*"Here, Louie!"*

That's all I have to say, and Louie comes running, even outdoors on a nice day. Here's how I train my cats to come when I call.

Start feeding him his wet meals at the same time everyday. When he's shows up to eat, say "Here, Louie," even if he's only a few feet away. When he reaches you, say, "Good boy, Louie!" and place the meal in front of him. Pet him and let him eat. Do this with every meal or special treat you give him. Soon, he will associate your call with eating and will be very motivated to show up.

**DID YOU KNOW?**

A cat will walk in the direction of whatever he wants. Whether it's play, food, or outside walks, he'll walk in that direction and stay in the area he gets those things while looking directly in your eyes. If he walks to you and stays near you, he probably wants to be petted and massaged. When he hurriedly walks away from you, he's most likely trying to show you what he wants.
He'll also hang out where he was last brushed or played with to see if he'll get brushed or played with again. He'll look at you then at his brush or toy.

**HELPFUL HINT**

Ask your cat what he wants, then follow him to where he leads you.

When your cat comes pretty dependable for his wet meals, start calling him when he's a few feet away. Graduate by calling when he's in another room. Choose times like when he's walking towards you and likely to reach you. This helps build habit and success. Say "Here, Louie!" Pet, then feed him when he arrives.

Make him earn his food by allowing you to touch him before he gets it as well. When he's doing pretty well on short distances, start calling him at unexpected times, such as naps, but only when he's going to get a really good reward such as his afternoon walk or his favorite toy.

Say the same words in same style every time so that he becomes conditioned to expect only goodness *any time* he hears that particular tone and combination.

In the first few months, do not pick up or hold a cat who comes to your call. Let him walk freely on the ground unless he asks you specifically to be picked up. The more you let a cat have his freedom when he comes when called, the more likely he'll walk to you again. As time goes by, he may not mind being picked up and held, even when he didn't ask.

After your cat is coming for wet meals he'll be ready for a few nonfood rewards when you call him. Use whatever your cat is enticed by: praise and petting, play, massage, catnip or a walk outside. Continue to say "Here, Louie" before wet meals everyday.

# OUTSIDE/INSIDE

*Most cats, when they are Out want to be In, and vice versa, and often simultaneously.*

—LOUIS J. CAMUTI, D.V.M.

When I take Louie and Marvin on their outside walks, they stay in the yard and come when called. They run to the house when they see cars and strangers and walk back into the house on their own accord. I don't have to chase them down or carry them all over the place because I taught them to behave outside.

Some shelters insist that the people who adopt cats from them do not let them outside. I can understand that. They've seen lots of lost, stolen, injured and dead cats because of outside hazards. But you can take your cat outside in relative safety by teaching him to avoid danger *and* stay in the yard.

Some cats can be taken on outside walks. Some cats can even be trusted to be alone for a few minutes.

Trained outside walks can help in many ways:

1. Make him more stress tolerant. Walking and fresh air help relieve stress.

2. Gets him familiar with his surroundings. He'll know where to go in the event that he accidentally gets outside.

3. A great way to reward indoor training for using the scratching post and for coming when called.

4. Being outdoors often alleviates the worst behavior problems—problems that lead some cats to mistreatment, abandonment or euthanasia.

## THE RIGHT CIRCUMSTANCES FOR TRAINING?

Supervised outside walks can be fun and very beneficial to

## SHOPPING LIST

### FOR OUTSIDE WALKS

✓ brightly colored cat collar with safety release, bell and phone number (write your phone number with permanent ink or add a tag)
✓ cat harness
✓ light-weight leash
✓ industrial squirt bottle and/or Super Soaker squirt gun
✓ cat treats or wet cat food

### OPTIONAL

✓ empty soda pop can with pennies taped inside
✓ cat tattooed with registered number—strongly recommended

### FOR INDOORS-ONLY CATS

✓ kitty oats (grown indoors)
✓ hairball remedy
✓ extra cat tree / post
✓ catnip
✓ extra litter box
✓ raw foods

### OPTIONAL

✓ bird feeder
✓ cat kennel

### RECOMMENDED READING

✓ *The City Cat*, by Roz Riddle
✓ *The Indoor Cat*, by Patricia Curtis

⚠️ **DON'T TAKE HIM OUTSIDE**

- At dark or near dark (twilight)
- When there's a moving van or vehicle with a trunk or window left open and unattended nearby
- On these holidays or the day before: Halloween, New Years Eve, Fourth of July, Cinco de Mayo, or any holiday that has fire crackers
- Right after any misbehavior. Going outside is a favorite reward. Don't reward bad behavior.
- If weed killer has recently been applied. Contact manufacturer for when lawn is safe for pets.

 **TRUE STORY**

My four-year-old Lincoln is far too aggressive against our neighbor's cat, Gray Baby. When I've tried taking Lincoln outside, Gray Baby shows up and Lincoln takes off and beats up our neighbor's cat (who's bigger). My other cats don't feel that way about Gray Baby, only Lincoln. I had to stop taking him outside. I'm keeping him inside and may try again next year. If I do, I'll pick a really super cold day so he'll have to stay close. (Such a mean mommy!)

cats and cat owners, but only if you have the proper cat, setting and time.

*Not just any cat can be taken on outside walks.* If your cat likes to fight or has been brought up in the streets, he may not take to this type of training well. Try keeping him in the house for several months. Then, if possible, begin training on an exceptionally cold day so that he'll only want to be out a few minutes.

If the cat is an extremely fast runner, or doesn't like to be touched or held, he won't be a good candidate for outside walks. If you live near heavy traffic or you don't have a yard you should probably keep your cat indoors. Or maybe there are predatory animals around. (See the Indoor-Only Cat section at the end of this chapter.)

If you have a kitten, consider keeping the kitten indoors for about a year to get him very used to routine. This can really help keep him closer to home when he goes on walks.

This training will start at about five minutes a session a day per cat. The time the cat will stay outside depends on how much he violates your orders during certain phases of training. Try to do outside walks daily. If you can only take the cat outside during the weekend, you may have a problem with declawed cats. Once they get used to outside walks, they may require one every day. The stress of being inside may make them pee outside the litter box. If you can't walk the declawed cat daily, you may not want to start this training.

## TRAINING

### BEFORE YOU BEGIN

The attitude you must convey to your cat is that going outside is his privilege, not his right. This training is geared for that attitude.

Ideally, your cat should live inside the house for quite a few months. You need to make the cat or kitten dependent upon you before going outside. During this time, feed wet meals at the same time each day so he learns when to expect them. Train him to come when called as outlined in the Basic Training.

Cats are creatures of habit—once they get used to being fed the same time, they'll come inside, even if it's a nice day.

Outside training requires a harness, leash, and a collar with a bell. Also, I highly recommended tattooing any cat who goes out. (See the appendix Products and Resources.)

Let your neighbors know that you have a cat and that you will be training him to stay in your yard. Tell them that your cat is not allowed in anybody else's yard but his own. If by chance your cat goes in a neighbor's yard, let them know to shoo him away. Or to call and let you know he's there.

Check that your cat's rabies vaccinations are up to date. Your local laws may require additional vaccines as well.

If you don't have a fence, set up some flags or stones to mark the boundaries your cat is to stay within.

Get a lure toy you can leave outside. Keep a spray bottle to stop cat fights. Children's pump-up squirt guns or industrial spray bottles are my favorites. The Super Soaker shoots pretty far. The longer stream lets you hide behind the bushes, waiting to ambush when he violates the rules. A spray bottle or two may be to have stationed around the house as backup arsenal. You'll use water later in the training.

Stick to a single session a day during the first several months or he'll pester you until you take him out a second time, then a third and so on. Later you'll be able to take him outside more than once a day if you want. But for now, he needs to respect.

To avoid a cat waking you up for his outside walk, wait until after 10:00 AM to start his outside walk. Always take him out during the daylight, never at night or in the twilight.

**HELPFUL HINTS**

When he walks up to you on his own, pet him and praise him. Pick him up if he wants. Let him go again for at least a few minutes even if it's time to come in. You always want to reward his coming to you.

Open the door and give him a chance to go in on his own.

**TRUE STORY**

I kept Marvin in the house a whole year before beginning outside training. By delaying his outdoor privileges, he is more cautious and stays pretty close to home.

## PHASE ONE

Phase one takes about three days. Its purpose is to give the cat a good first impression of the outdoors. For this phase, pick a quiet time so that the cat is less overwhelmed. Also, choose a time shortly before your cat usually takes a nap because he'll be tired and more likely to stay close to home. For most cats this seems to be between 10:00 AM and 3:00 PM. Later, we'll use noisier and busier times.

When it's time to go out, call "Here, Louie!" even if he's already by the door. Praise him while you put on his harness and leash. Make sure he's also wearing a collar with a bell just in case he slips out of the harness.

Tell him it's time to go outside but that it's also "time to scratch." Put him on his scratching post. As soon as a claw goes in, praise him as you pick him up and carry him through the doorway. (You need to carry him so he knows you're in control. This will also change later.) Set him down facing the house a few feet outside the door. Pet him now so that right away he starts getting used to being touched outside.

Let him walk around and sniff at things while you keep hold of his leash. *Every few minutes, go to him, pick him up, pet him, say his name and put him down facing the house.* This helps avoid teaching the cat to run from you. He will learn to run and hide if you take him inside as soon as you get your hands on him. Remember, first impressions are important, start getting him used to be handled and approached right away. You want to be able to touch or pick up your cat anytime he's outside.

Don't drag him by the leash and harness or he'll learn to escape. Cats can escape most harnesses. Once a cat finds out he can get out of one, he'll escape all the time. Stay close by so that you can get your hands on him at any given time. It's okay to step on the leash should he suddenly bolt away from you but get your hands on him immediately (because the harness won't hold him). If he bolts, puts your hands on him and see if he'll calm down. But if he's too ready to run off again, take him inside. Give him a treat and try again tomorrow. It's not a good idea to take a cat inside as soon as you get your hands on him while he's in his own yard, but bolting needs to be discouraged until he learns the yard boundaries.

Praise him whenever he walks towards the house or you. Play with him near the house using the lure toy you've been keeping on the porch. Let him know that staying near or going in the house is a good thing.

Keep the sessions short and avoid letting him near the yard boundary for these first three days. You don't want to have to say "no" during this part of the training.

Later on, he'll learn to come back indoors on his own. Now, though, you need to keep his outside walk short because he's not likely to walk in on his own. You'll have to pick him up. Don't call him when it's time to go in, go to him and pick him up. If the cat stays calm in your arms, carry him around for several seconds before you take him in so that he doesn't associate getting picked up with going inside. If he gets antsy, however, take him in immediately.

As soon as he's inside, praise him, and remove his harness and leash and bell. Tell him how good he is to be home. Give him a treat or serve a wet meal if it's mealtime. Coming home always deserves a special food treat, no matter how he acted outside.

Most cats love the outdoors but some are frightened by it at first. He may act like he doesn't like the outside at all. If he freaks out once he gets outside, try using a lure toy to distract his fear. Don't talk to him unless he loosens up or wants back in the house. Then open the door, praise him and let him slink back inside. Tell him how good he is to come inside no matter how scaredy-cat he seems. Give him a treat and try phase one for the next day or two. If he doesn't like it any bet-

## HELPFUL HINTS

Choose only one door of the house to let your cat out of. It's easier to manage just one door.

Allow him to walk inside through any door.

If your home has other doors he can go out of, don't let him use the front door to walk out of. You'll have less trouble with your cats when you reserve that door for visitors.

If he gets out the door on his own without your permission, get him back inside the house as soon as possible. Don't let him get away with it even once.

## HINTS TO HELP HIM AVOID DANGER

Show fear when a car approaches. Say, "Ooooh! Car. Be careful!" in a frightened tone of voice. Pick him up and walk quickly to the house. Put him down facing the street instead of the house so that he can look at what you are afraid of. Keep a hand on him. Sound shaky and nervous until the sound of the car disappears.

If a stranger walks by your property, be quiet but walk swiftly toward your house. Then turn around and watch until the person has gone by. Your cat will watch and pick up on your reactions. You may not want to act too scared in this case or the stranger might think you're weird. Also, by being quiet, you won't draw unnecessary attention to a cat who's supposed to be hiding from strangers.

ter, don't force it. Let him stay indoors. See the Indoor-Only Cat section later in this chapter.

### PHASE TWO

In this phase he'll learn where the property lines exist and that if he crosses them too much, it will stop his walk for the day. He'll also come to understand that walking to you or staying on his own turf earns him extra time outside.

Gradually change his walk to a busier and noisier time of the day. This will make him more aware of the dangers outside. Sometimes the commotion alone will make him stay near the house. Ideally, time the training sessions to end right before it's time for a wet meal.

Begin by taking your cat outside just as in phase one. But this time, after you set him down outside and pet him, let go of the leash. Let him go wherever he wants. And again, as in phase one, every few minutes, go to him and pick him up, pet him and set him back down again, facing the house.

Whenever he gets near the yard boundary, watch closely and be near him. The instant he steps on the sidewalk or outside any boundary, say "no." Stop him from going further by walking in front of him and gently force him back into his yard by pushing him *gently* with your hand. If he won't get back to his own yard, pick him up and return him to just inside his property line. Say "good boy" as soon as he's back in bounds.

Stay close to him as he roams around the yard. If he approaches the line again, say something like, "Uh-uh," or "Hey! I'm watching you," but do not say his name. If he crosses the boundary again, then again put him back inside his yard. Take him inside if he crosses a third time.

A good time to take a cat inside the house when you catch him in someone else's yard and he makes no attempt to run to you or run back home. If he runs back into his yard before you can catch him, let him stay out a little bit longer.

Remember, don't take him inside when he walks to you. When he walks up to you, tell him he's a very good boy and pet him. Pick him up only if he wants you to and set him back down *before* he wants down.

When it's time to go inside and he doesn't walk inside on his own, either wait until he's crossed a yard boundary or try a lure toy and see if he'll follow it indoors. If he does, continue to play with him once he's inside.  If all else fails, go to him and carry him around a few seconds. If he gets antsy, take him inside right away. As soon as he's inside, let him go gently and give him a treat. Remove the harness and leash.

Your cat will need to make mistakes on all sides of the yard. He'll need to experience being yelled at, gently pushed and carried back from all sides if your property. He needs to learn where the lines exist by making mistakes.

Make sure you respond each time he trespasses, either by putting him back in the yard or taking him in the house. Letting him get away with it without making him get back in his own yard can set the training back a few weeks.

Whenever you call for him outside, have his most special food ready, or a very favorite toy. Praise him as soon as he shows up, even if it's 10 minutes later after you called. Use special rewards when he comes while being called when he's outside.

If he likes to bolt for several days in this phase, he may not be a good candidate for this training. Keeping him inside the house for a year, and getting him to come when called during that time, may help break his need to run.

Most cats will learn where the yard boundary is. When he continues to hesitate before crossing it for several days in a row, he's waiting to see if you're paying attention. So you know he knows, start cutting down to only allowing only two mistakes for a week or two.  And now it's time for phase three.

### PHASE THREE

In phase three you no longer need to use the leash and harness. Continue to use the collar and bell from now on, whenever he's outside.

When he scratches his post after you've asked him to, now let him *walk* out the door without being carried.

At the beginning of this off-leash training, warn him not to trespass when he approaches a property line. Stay close. If he violates your verbal warning, take him inside right away, even just once. Try to get your hands on him as soon as he has crossed the boundary. Do this for several weeks.

As your cat gets better at staying in the yard, gradually let him go farther away from you. But keep him in sight. When he almost always respects the border while you're there, and is pretty good about coming when you call him outside, start letting him get out of your sight. At least make it so you're out of *his* sight. If you can spy on him, do it. If not, only leave for a few seconds. Gradually increase your time away to a few minutes and longer.

If you find he sneaks outside the boundaries when you aren't looking, hide on him. Then use scare tactics such as spraying water in his path or throwing something near him the second he steps out of bounds. A snow ball or an empty pop can with a few pennies inside can help startle him too. If he runs back into the yard on his own, let him stay out. If he refuses to go back, take him indoors.

As the weeks pass in phase three, you can relax again about the number of mistakes unless he starts making too many, then go back to one mistake. Sometimes you may want to give him another chance (as I like to do on a nice sunny day). Tell him, "Get back in the yard." If he walks back into the yard on his own, let him stay out. If not, go get him with the attitude, "You should have listened to me! You thought I was joking." And take him inside. Over time the cat will learn that staying within the property lines and walking to you earns him more time outside.

The more he stays in the yard with your back turned, the longer you can leave him on his own. As you become more confident that he'll stay in the yard, you can just come out to check on him occasionally. It may take a few months of daily training so that he can be trusted to be on his own for very short periods.

When the cat walks into the house on his own, you can start to let him back outside again, within a few minutes, on the same day if he wants. On bad weather days a cat will probably want in, then out, then in and out again. When you're ready to keep him inside for the day, give him his treat.

Once in a great while you can use scruffing when he crosses the *street*. Save this last resort punishment for when he continues to cross the street in spite of your warning him not to leave the yard. Carry him back to your yard and release the scruffing grip but carry him indoors immediately. Don't forget to reward and praise him for coming home. Only use this method on very rare occasions and only when he crosses into a very dangerous area of the outdoors. If your cat continues to go out into the street fairly often, try phase two again using a harness and leash. Resorting to scruffing a cat outside more than twice might mean that this cat is not a good candidate for outside training.

If he leaves your yard while you're not there, praise him when he returns to the yard or door, even if he's been gone for awhile. As soon as you realize he's missing, go looking for him. Walk by the houses adjacent to your house and call his name. You may find him two houses away, and when he sees you, he'll likely start running back home. Sound and act surprised and happy to see him. If he runs to you sound extremely happy and grateful. But if he runs in the opposite direction, go after him as you say "no." Catch him and sound irritated at him until he's back inside the yard boundary and take him inside immediately.

As always, once your cat is back in the house, whether he was carried or walked back in on his own, he needs to know he's always a good boy for coming home. It's time for his wet meal or treat. "Louie's home!"

## SPECIAL CONSIDERATIONS

### MULTIPLE CATS

If you are training more than one cat, train them outside separately until at least one of them is at the stage where you can trust him unattended for at least five minutes. If you have to take one of them indoors, you need to be able to trust the other one while you're gone.

### DECLAWED CATS

If your cat is declawed, try to be very regular about sessions. Even after phase three training, stay outside with your declawed cat. Do not leave him alone, even for a minute. Your presence provides some protection against an attack from a dog or other animal.

### INDOOR-ONLY CAT

Tips for keeping your indoor cat healthy and happy:

- Compensate for the lack of fresh grass by feeding him kitty oats. If you use a commercial hairball remedy, use the maximum recommended dosage. (See the Yucky Stuff chapter for more on hairball remedies.)

- Add raw organic meats, vegetables and grains to his diet at least twice a week to make up for the insects and critters he would normally eat outside. Feed mostly wet foods.

- Put cat beds in sunlit windows. A bird feeder outside the window can help him pass the time.

- Increase your playtime with him, and play with him regularly.

• Let your cat jump on sturdy desks, file cabinets, bookcases and sofas to increase his livable space. Remove breakables and slippery things from places the cat can jump. He may accidentally knock things down or fall after landing on something slippery.

• If your cat was used to going outside but can't now, try to ease his stress. Supplement his meals with vitamins. And give him catnip. Add an extra litter box and a new cat post or cat tree no matter how many you already have. They're great for exercise and relieving the stress of living indoors.

• Install an outdoor kennel. Chain link is a good material. Put a scratching post or cat tree, dog house and catnip plants in the kennel if you can. If possible, install a cat door to the kennel from inside the house. Use a padlock to keep curious strangers out.

**RELATED CHAPTERS**

• *Basic Training*
• *Scratching Posts, Exercise and Play*
• *Diet*
• *Yucky Stuff*
• *Neighbors*
• *Lost and Found*

# AGGRESSION

*To err is human, To purr is feline.*

—ROBERT BYRNE

**SHOPPING LIST**

✓ large catnip-
   filled stuffed toy
   (aggression toy)
✓ industrial squirt bottle
✓ cat vitamins

**OPTIONAL**

✓ recording of birds and outdoor wildlife

 **WARNING**

This chapter does
not deal with
behavior where a cat bites
and draws blood or attacks
with teeth and claws with
intent to do serious harm. If
the cat is and has been
super-aggressive I recommend
you seek the help of a
qualified behaviorist.

Sudden aggressive behavior
could be due to abuse, a bad
scare or a medical problem. If
his sudden aggression doesn't
subside in a few minutes, call
the veterinarian. A cat who
suddenly turns aggressive
might be seriously sick or
injured.

The average, healthy cat adopted from a shelter is not aggressive and should not hurt you under normal circumstances. Some cats will occasionally bite or scratch at you when irritated or handled roughly. And some may act mean toward other cats in the house or neighbor cats. But generally, your average healthy cat should not hurt you or others.

In this chapter I'll give you tips on how to curb aggressive behavior against both people and other cats.

## CAUSES OF AGGRESSIVE BEHAVIOR

There are several possible reasons for aggressive behavior.

- Lack of handling as a kitten: frequent handling of a kitten is a very important part of bringing up a friendly and gentle cat. When a kitten is not handled much or at all, he can grow up disliking being touched and preferring to be left alone. Such a cat may resist handling with a nip or a slap with his paws. A big part of behavior problems with feral cats is the lack of human handling at a critical stage in the cat's life.

- Mistreatment or abuse: if a cat or kitten is treated very roughly to the point that it suffers pain and discomfort, he will learn to resist human contact.

- Illness or injury: ill or injured cats, like people, can be quite irritable and even hostile. Even an innocent touch can cause pain or discomfort. A thyroid problem is just one condition known to trigger aggressive behavior in cats.

Take your cat to a veterinarian to determine if your cat's aggression is caused by being sick or injured.

• Rough handling or play

• Threatening or frightening situation: cats are cautious creatures. Your cat may be frightened of something as obvious as a strange dog or as trivial as a slammed door. In either case, if you're holding him when he bolts, he might scratch you trying to get away. If it's an extremely frightening situation, he might even bite.

• Stressful living environment: a stressed cat is more likely to bite or scratch or, more often, become skittish. Stress can be caused by many different factors. Your home may not be large enough for your family and your cats. Or too noisy—certain noise levels or sounds may trigger aggressive behavior. If your cat was used to regular time outside and now stays indoors, this change can cause stress.

• Diet: certain foods, malnutrition and vitamin deficiencies can also trigger aggression.

• Old age: old cats sometimes get grumpy. As long as he's not hurting anyone, let him growl or hiss.

• Declawing: declawed cats are often more quick to bite. (See the special section on declawed cats near the end of this chapter.)

• Lack of exercise

• Boredom

## AGGRESSIVE BEHAVIOR AGAINST HUMANS

If your new kitten attacks you, it probably won't hurt. But never encourage this behavior—you don't want him grow up thinking that climbing up people's legs is acceptable behavior. If he attacks you when he's an adult, it is definitely not cute. He must learn to attack only his own belongings.

• If he just growls or hisses, just walk away.

**TRUE STORY**
Every time I sing, Bob comes to me, cries and nips me on the leg. If I continue to sing, he continues to nip at me until I stop singing. He doesn't exhibit this mild aggression to any of the many singers that have sung in our home. . . just to me. I won't try to change Bobs' honesty. I'm a pretty bad singer. Now I sing in the shower—sounds better there too.

Louie takes his aggression out on an aggression toy.

- If he actually bites you or scratches, say, "Ouch!" immediately and sound hurt even if it really didn't hurt. Rub your bite and walk away.

- If he's a kitten and you're confident you won't get hurt, pick him up and set him down pointing away from you. Walk away. If he persists, lock him in the bathroom for five minutes. If he's still feeling feisty when he comes out, have a lure toy ready and play with him when you let him out.

- Watch for his warning signs of anger or agitation. Pay attention to how he holds his ears, tail and posture before he attacks. Watch his eyes and mouth. If you see an attack coming try distracting him with a lure toy. Or push an "aggression toy" onto him. Give him something that he can kick and bite. Use a large fuzzy catnip toy, stuffed animal sprayed with catnip. Or make your own: Stuff a tube of strong, snaggy fabric with polyester fiberfill and dried catnip. Sew the ends shut. It should be long enough for him to bite and kick at the same time. A terry cloth sock works well.

- Handle with care. Almost any cat will defend itself against rough handling. Even if your cat only scratches or bites in that situation, stop doing it. Rough play is not a good idea anyway. You want your cat calm and happy, not riled up.

- Don't use your hands to play with your cat. Use a lure toy. When cats play, they use their teeth and claws.

- For cats who turn aggressive because of certain noises, avoid those noises when you're around if possible. However, at the same time you'll need to get the cat more used to human noise by playing music or television every day. Don't let him always be in a quiet environment. He needs to be exposed to normal human sounds to get more used to living with them.

- Add cat vitamin supplements to help alleviate moodiness. (Other ways to alleviate stress are in the Litter Box Blues chapter.)

- Keep his nails trimmed. Kitten's claws are very sharp and will easily cut through your skin. Adult claws can do even more serious damage.

- Watch his diet. Sometimes, a specific food can cause allergic reactions that can lead to angry spells. Tuna, yeast and hormone-injected meats have been known to do that in some cats.

- Do not hold a cat when he's likely to be suddenly frightened, such as when meeting a new cat or dog, walking near an appliance making noise, etc.

- If you get a kitten that's really aggressive and doesn't respond to training, take him back and get another. If your new adult cat is aggressive, consider returning him right away. Do not adopt a cat you think is dangerous.

## CAT FIGHT?

Cats who live together play together, often by pretending to fight. Just because they growl and tumble doesn't mean they're not playing. A serious cat fight has very quick movements, is very violent, includes high screeching sounds (not just howling), often produces blood on at least one cat and doesn't last very long. Usually tumbling and slower movements signify playing. This advice is intended only for nonserious cat fights.

If you would like your cats to get a long a little bit better, and have more fun with each other, here are some things to do:

- While they are calm and relaxed, rub one cat and then the other. His scent will linger on your hands. This helps get the cats more familiar with each other.

- For one week, put a snap-away collar *with a bell* on the

## IS IT A SERIOUS FIGHT OR ARE THEY PLAYING?

I called one of my foster cat's homes to see how things were going. Ruthie's new owner was worried that she and her other cat were "fighting." I asked the owner if the fights were so fast that you couldn't see their paws move. No. I asked if they can't stand to be next to each other. No. They touch noses once in a while. I asked where they slept. Both on the same bed. I had to tell her the cats were just playing.

### TRUE STORY

Our Louie wouldn't hurt a soul and is very shy. But he has such a passion for playing that if another cat enters the room during his playtime with me, he will attack him. Not in any serious way, mind you. . . yet, at no other time is Louie aggressive. (By the way, he always loses when he fights— but don't tell Louie that.)

most aggressive cat. This warns a more timid cat that the bully is coming.

- During mealtimes, feed the most aggressive eater first. Don't give him an additional excuse to fly off the handle.

- Cats will play by wrestling with each other. It could look like a real cat fight to someone who doesn't know that's how cats play. And they may howl and talk to each other as if it's serious. But it probably isn't. I usually just let them go on because I know they're not going to hurt each other. If I think a confrontation is growing more serious, I disrupt it by waving a lure toy and get them engaged in playing. Occasionally I may just throw a pillow near them. To further distract them, I sometimes turn on loud music before getting the toy out.

- If one cat is being hurt and is crying out in pain, and, if you know you won't get hurt, separate them. Pick up and comfort the cat being picked on. Ask him if he's all right. Ignore the bully. Don't say his name or make eye contact for awhile.

- If a fight breaks out, tell them to both "knock it off" in a serious voice. If it looks like somebody might get really hurt, say nothing. Use a squirt bottle. Be careful not to squirt their heads. Try to prevent fights from escalating by stepping in sooner next time.

- If you have a real problem cat who is constantly bullying everyone, put him in a boarding kennel for a week. He's likely to reflect on how good his life was before "going on vacation." When you bring him back home, confine him to a bathroom for another week. Allow him back into the household when the other cats are napping or are outside. Keep a bell on him for another week.

- If serious cat fights persist, consider finding another home for the bully. If he's not declawed, look for a place he can be outside, too.

## NEIGHBORHOOD CATS

Some indoor cats become agitated when they see a strange cat outside. Keep a scratching post near his favorite window. When he starts to heat up, direct him to the post. Instead of reprimanding him, tell him how brave he is for protecting the house. You may even want to place a cat bed near the window so he feels like he has an important job.

The most serious confrontations often occur when your cat is outside and unexpectedly encounters someone else's cat. Most cats try to avoid a fight but there are a few who want to pick a fight with everything they see. If they do start fighting, break it up with a spray bottle or squirt gun. Spray the water *between* the brawling cats. Avoid their heads and stay as far away from the action as you can. If the fight is serious, even direct hits of water won't break it up. Keep your distance. When the fight is over, squirt at the strange cat until he's out of the yard.

Never touch a strange cat, or, your cat, when he's angry. *Also, never use any part of your body to intervene*—you could be seriously hurt. Keep your distance until things calm down. Even the most loving cat may not recognize you when he's enraged.

Don't make too much of a first fight. Cats get used to each other, and they may actually start to hang out together.

## SPECIAL CONSIDERATIONS

### DECLAWED CATS

An aggression problem with a declawed cat can take longer to turn around. You may have to accept more frequent biting and other aggressive behavior. But he should improve over time. To help him learn:

• Offer your hands to him when you don't think he'll bite. Rub his chin but be careful, declawed cats can be moody and unpredictable. It may take several months before he learns to stop biting you and he will learn if he knows you will never respond to his bites with violence or handle him roughly.

- When he bites you, say "ouch!" and pull your hand away. If he doesn't release your hand, push it into his mouth. This forces the cat to open his mouth and release you. Since he's a declawed cat, I give him a second chance before I walk away.

- Let him hiss at other cats. If he hisses at you, walk away. If he hisses at you when you are outside, take him in immediately.

## IF YOU'RE STILL HAVING TROUBLES

If the ideas here don't help enough, you may need a professional cat behaviorist. A tranquilizer may help a cat through a stressful period in his life. Ask your veterinarian about it, or consider a new home for him where he can spend more time outside.

## WHAT NOT TO DO

If you are considering declawing and/or teeth pulling, I urge you to reconsider. A cat without claws or teeth will be more stressed and more trouble to care for than the average cat at your local animal shelter.

# LITTER BOX BLUES

*If the essential core of the person is denied or suppressed, he gets sick sometimes in obvious ways, sometimes in subtle ways, sometimes immediately, sometimes later.*

—ABRAHAM MASLOW

More than half the phone calls I receive from cat owners are about cat urine problems. Cat urine is one of the most potent smells in the entire world. And it's no wonder that this problem causes even the best of us to have second thoughts about cats.

Cat urine can destroy practically anything. If the problem goes on long enough, the stench will permanently damage sofas, and even floorboards and dry wall.

If you keep a clean litter box and your cat pees outside the box then something is wrong. In this chapter I'll give you help with litter box problems and tips on how to prevent them in the future.

## CAUSES OF LITTER BOX PROBLEMS

Stress is the major cause of litter box problems. Cats get stressed out for the same reasons that people do. These reasons include:

**Illness or pain.** Usually the first sign that a clawed cat is sick is that he pees outside the box. Ailments such as constipation, infection, kidney stones, bad thyroid, epilepsy, depression, pain, impacted anal glands as well as urinary tract problems such as feline urologic syndrome (FUS) frequently cause cats to pee outside the box.

**Poor diet and lack of exercise.** A dry-food-only, unbalanced or unvaried diet can contribute to kidney, liver or bladder problems. Allergic reactions to certain foods may also prompt depression or litter box problems.

### SHOPPING LIST

✓ see veterinarian for exam, get tests
✓ urine neutralizer
✓ extra food bowl
✓ cat litter, different brands
✓ extra litter box or two
✓ homemade food
✓ lure toy
✓ tall, sturdy scratching post (clawed cats only)

### OPTIONAL

✓ carpet runner, laundry basket
✓ large piece of cardboard or office mat that chairs roll on
✓ corner litter box
✓ disposable litter boxes or cardboard boxes for litter test
✓ Odor Eliminator bags (neutralizer that naturally absorb odors, "re-charged" by exposing them to the sun for a day; see appendix.)
✓ black light

### SHOPPING LIST FOR DECLAWED CATS

✓ see section later in chapter

### NOTE:

Litter Box Blues is about urinating on carpet. For spraying and pooping problems, see the *Miscellaneous Problems* chapter.

**WARNINGS**

If you are pregnant, do not handle cat litter. See warnings in the Safety chapter.

Do not reprimand a cat for peeing outside the litter box!

If your cat cries or strains while peeing, tries to pees more than twice in an hour, he should see a veterinarian immediately!

## WHICH CAT IS THE CULPRIT?

In multicat households, make sure you identify the right cat. Some veterinarians can offer pills each cat can take to discolor his urine and to find that color with a black light.

Most cats like to urinate when they first get up in the morning. Get up a little earlier some morning to spy on them .

Use a video camera to record events while you're not there. I know a cat owner who did that and discovered a neighbor's cat was coming into the house through the cat door.

**Change.** Keeping an outdoor cat indoors, moving to a new house, extended vacations, a new dog can be very stressful to some cats. Declawed cats often have a more difficult time with disruption in their daily routine and environment.

**Declawing.** Perhaps because declawing makes it difficult for a cat to cover its waste, declawed cats have a much higher frequency of more serious litter box problems.

**Poor environment.** Violence, overcrowding, loneliness, boredom, sharp smells, loud noises or a couple who argues all the time all make the cat's life more stressful.

**Litter box.** If the box isn't kept clean or is placed in a bad location, the cat may not use it. The new electronic litter boxes, which rake the solids into a tray, may frighten and intimidate some cats to the point that they refuse to use it.

**Feral cat (wild cat).** Feral cats are not domesticated. If one has been used to living outside and is brought in the house, he may retaliate by peeing outside the box. It's his way of telling you he's not meant to be there.

**Territorial challenges.** Some cats get upset by seeing or smelling a strange cat near their home.

**Bad chemistry.** Not every cat fits into every home. Some cats have trouble adjusting to the wrong set of people, cats, dogs or other pets.

## PREVENTING LITTER BOX PROBLEMS

The most important thing to remember is that healthy, *clawed* cats rarely have a litter box problem. As a quick checklist, is your cat:

**?** Eating two to three wet meals a day? Eating high quality foods?

**?** Eating a wide variety of foods?

**?** Spending daily time with you? Getting attention every day? Cats like routine. A daily, consistent schedule for scratching post, meals, outdoor and play time can help reduce stress and build confidence.

**?** Living with too many? Overcrowding can result in territorial pressures.

**?** Getting exercise? Is he using the scratching post?

**?** Confusing heaps of dirty laundry or foul-smelling objects, such as tennis shoes, as litter boxes? Keep dirty laundry in hampers and shoes tucked away.

## WHEN YOUR CAT PEES OUTSIDE THE LITTER BOX

Although there are no guarantees with litter box problems, there are at least four things you can do that should help.

### *TAKE HIM TO THE DOCTOR*

Cats don't normally pee outside the box unless something is wrong. Even if you've just had a baby or moved, the onset of litter box problems may be due to illness. Never assume the problem is "just behavioral."

• To make sure the problem isn't medical, take him to the veterinarian. Before you go, inspect the litter box for the condition of his stools and urine and for any blood.

• If you've already been to a veterinarian, you may want to try again. Consider trying a "holistic" veterinarian who uses acupuncture, chiropractic techniques, herbs or homeopathic home remedies.

• So that there are no surprises, call two or three different offices and ask how much the exam, urine test, blood tests and medicine will cost. No matter how old your cat is, get a urine test! Do not assume that just because your veterinarian *looked* at the cat, he's okay. Ask the veterinarian how the urine can be collected. (See the sidebar: Collecting Urine.)

• The vet may want to do a blood test, especially if the cat is

---

**COLLECTING URINE**

If you think about collecting the urine yourself at home, be careful that the urine is fresh when tested. You must put it on ice right away and take it in immediately. Also, the urine sample must be clean. The cat needs to pee in a clean specimen cup, or in a clean empty box. Sometimes people will use Styrofoam packing material as a clean temporary "litter."

It's easier to have the veterinarian collect it to guarantee freshness.

Ask the veterinarian to squeeze the cat's bladder rather than insert a catheter.

## TRUE STORY

One woman called me and was sure she needed to hire me. Her cat was urinating outside the box because of her new three-month-old baby.

I told her I didn't think her problem was "behavioral." Most urine problems aren't. The cat is either sick or stressed.

I was right. The owner called me up later and told me the cat almost died from a blockage in the bladder. The problem had been brewing for several months but the owner mistook the cat's urination as a sign of "behavioral" problems.

## NEUTRALIZER PRODUCT LIST

These neutralizers are found at most pet stores, mail order and some hardware stores. Read the labels for instructions on how to use. Many other products are on the market, all could not be included here.

• AOE Animal Odor Eliminator
• Mom's Odor Eliminator sacks
• Nature's Miracle
• Pet Preference

older. This test will detect liver, kidney or thyroid problems and will be useful as a baseline to evaluate changes in the cat's condition as time passes.

• Declawed cats should have their toes checked for infections or any other amputee-related problem.

• If at all possible, avoid feeding dry food altogether when a litter box problem exists. If the veterinarian prescribes a specific dry food and it contains ethoxyquin, ask for alternatives. If feeding dry food is necessary, ask him about foods such as Felidae, Neura Special Diet, Wysong Uretic or prescription foods by Nature's Recipe, which are naturally preserved and are designed for urinary tract health.

• If the veterinarian prescribes an antibiotic, steroid, antidepressant or tranquilizer, find out what side effects and risks are associated with each medicine.

## HANDLE WITH CARE

• Don't yell at him or rub his nose in the urine. Don't reprimand him. Don't show anger. Don't talk to your cat as if he is bad. But don't say his name or "poor baby" either. Just say "oh, no" or nothing at all. Act like he's sick. Treating him like he's bad will make matters worse.

• Pick him up, take him to the litter box right away. Do not put him outside. Set up a confinement room with a litter box and bowl of water, as described in the Newcomer chapter, and lock him in.

• In his new room, talk gently while showing him where things are. Have a wet meal ready and spend some time with him before he's left alone. Turn on a radio and light.

• Keep the cat in the room whenever you can't watch him— even when you are on the phone or doing the dishes. It's best to keep him confined for the next two weeks. Being in a small room will force the cat to use his box.

## NEUTRALIZE THE URINE

Because urine can permanently damage anything porous, thoroughly neutralize a urine spot on carpet or furniture. It's very important to not leave an odor that will attract a cat to pee there again.

If you're not sure exactly where the spot is, find it by feeling with a paper towel or by walking around in some old socks. Sniff the spot to make sure you found urine. It sounds gross, but if you don't get on your hands and knees to find it now, you won't have to get on your hands and knees to find it later. . . and, you'll just want to move away instead.

Commercial neutralizers made especially for pet urine are inexpensive but vinegar also works as a stopgap measure. Buy the commercial stuff and apply it as soon as you can.

Sop up as much as you can with a sponge or paper towels. Apply the neutralizer according to the directions on the package. If they've peed on clothes or a pillow, wash objects with some of the neutralizer and let them dry. You may want to inject neutralizer into the sofa, but test it for color fastness first. Then cover the sofa and keep it covered until you know your cat's using his box again.

If the urine has penetrated the carpet pad, try injecting neutralizer under the carpet with a syringe. If you have to replace the carpet, apply a special paint sealer to the floorboards. If the urine damage is deep enough you may not get rid of the odor until you replace all affected floorboard and drywall.

You must get rid of all unneutralized urine spots in your house, even the old ones. A black light can help you find them. Also watch to see if your cat sniffs the floor. It could be an old spot.

Keep all pets away from the spot until the urine has been totally neutralized. Cover it with a laundry basket or a piece of furniture to allow it to dry. When the spot is dry, guard it

## HOW OFTEN DO I NEED TO CHANGE THE LITTER?

If you have one litter box per cat, as I recommend, you will probably need to change each box about once a week as well as scooping out the solids every day. If they use one box more than another, you'll need to change it more often. And you can change the other one less often so you can still average about once a week per box.

But if a box starts to smell, change it now. Read the cat litter bag/box for instructions as well.

## HELPFUL LITTER BOX HINTS

If your cat pees in a potted plant, cover the dirt with pine cones or decorative rocks.

If he pees on your bed, wash the bedding and neutralize mattress spots immediately. Later on, pet him or play with him on the bed.

Avoid putting a litter box directly on carpet so that if he reaches outside the box to scratch at the litter, he doesn't snag carpet. Protect your carpet with a carpet runner, carpet office mat or plain cardboard.

with rubber or plastic carpet runner (either right side up or knobby side up).

Some neutralizers work right away, but some take two weeks. After removing the guard, place a food bowl or carpet runner on the spot to keep it further inaccessible and to make him forget it was there. Don't use tin foil to cover it up because the foil crumples and your cat could choke on it.

## IMPROVE HIS LITTER BOX EXPERIENCE

Some cats won't go in the box because it's too dirty. Scoop solids and lift out wet spots daily. Keep the area around the box clean. Change the litter when it starts to smell, which is about a week per cat. (See the sidebar. Also see Litter Boxes Etc. for maintenance of litter boxes.)

Make sure you have enough litter boxes. Set up one litter box per cat, plus one extra.

If your home is too small for that many litter boxes, try to find a small litter box that fits snugly in a corner. These small triangular boxes are difficult to find but work surprisingly well for the size they take up. The corner boxes are very easy to clean and a great way to add more litter boxes without taking up a lot of space.

Put less litter in each box. Some cats will pee in a practically empty litter box.

If he's using scented litter, try nonscented litter; if he's using clay litter, try pellets. Let your cat decide what he likes.

Try different size boxes. Some cats like bigger boxes, some like smaller ones. The hardware or department stores have utility boxes larger than the average litter boxes. Some stores carry smaller boxes, such as the corner litter box. Older cats or kittens may need a lower, shorter box.

Try a covered litter box. Point the opening so he can see people or pets approaching. Or if you already have a covered box, try an uncovered one.

Location is important. Unless your cat is very old or very young, keep the litter boxes away from their food, scratching posts and beds. A bathroom or laundry room is usually a good place. Don't put it in a room he doesn't like to go in, or in an area that is heavily trafficked by dogs.

Remove the plastic liner if you are using one. Some cats don't like the liner.

Only touch a cat when he is inside the box is if he raises his hind end to pee over the edge of the box. Gently touch his rear end and hold it down. Don't say anything. Then buy a box with higher sides or a covered box. Protect the floor and wall with plastic.  Or place the litter box inside a large TV box with one side and the top cut out. Drape newspapers over the edges, replace as needed.

(See Litter Boxes Etc. for more information about litters, boxes, locations and maintenance.)

Note: if the litter is kept clean, then it's probably not the brand of litter. Something else is wrong when a cat stops using a litter box.

### MORE HELP

Choose ideas below that you think might help, considering your situation, time, patience, and budget.

- Stop feeding dry food or stop leaving it out in-between meals. If possible, feed only wet food, especially to old cats—they need all the moisture they can get. Add water to their wet food too.

- Add a pinch of fresh garlic to his food to help manage stress.

- Your cat may be allergic to some particular food or ingredient. Try more chicken and lamb-based foods, fresh meat or fish, and vegetables, as well as different grains like brown rice, corn, or wheat (preferably whole wheat).

- Withhold food products and supplements containing yeast

**DID YOU KNOW?**

A cat in the wild is meticulous about covering up his waste the closer he is to his nest.

for a month or until the urination problem is under control. Slowly add the yeast product back into his diet. If a reaction occurs he could be sensitive to some products containing yeast.

- Don't feed salt or salty foods that make him drink more water. Salt can strain already weary kidneys; besides, cats weren't designed to drink a lot of water.

- Add fiber to his diet. Use a hairball remedy. (See the Hair and Nails chapter.)

- Feed him roasted chicken necks twice a week. They have a lot of calcium.

- If you're desperate, stop feeding canned food altogether and feed only raw organic foods.

- An old cat may not be able to wait to be let outside or to make it down to the basement in the middle of the night. Put a litter box on each level of the house and near the room where he sleeps. Also keep a litter box on each level for a kitten until it is old enough to know its way around the house.

- Make sure you have a litter box indoors even if your cat is allowed outside. He needs a place that is always safe.

- Too many pets in too little space cause stress. Adding an outdoor kennel could provide some additional space and stress relief, especially if it's accessible from indoors. (See the Outside/Inside chapter.)

- If your cat is frightened by constant or frequent noise and commotion, try to set up a quiet place for him to retreat to. An open carrier case with a blanket in it is good. Playing music can help cover the noise of nearby construction or traffic.

- Don't leave dirty clothes or bad-smelling articles out, like shoes. Some cats will pee on rank-smelling stuff.

- Speak to other members in the household. Make sure everyone understands how to treat the cat. Ask them to help you with feeding the cat and cleaning up.

- Being an only cat may be difficult for many cats. But don't get a new cat until the litter box problem is fixed.

- Some cats only pee outside the box when their owners come home from vacation. Just in case, pay special attention to your cat when you get home. Before you look at the mail or listen to phone messages, spend time with him. Play with him. As soon as he uses his box, go to the kitchen and feed him a wet meal. If you will be gone for more than two days, get someone to visit your cat once a day.

- Eastern medicine hands-on remedies like Jin Shin Jyutsu or Tellington Touch may help. You can take lessons in using these techniques yourself.

- Contact a cat behaviorist for advice. Ask questions to assure yourself that she is qualified. A few behaviorists are listed in the back of this book. Many animal shelters can direct you to free help, or refer you to someone who knows about cat behavior problems.

- A cat door could be letting strange cats inside the house. Your cat may be intimidated by the intruder and use peeing as a way to mark his territory. The strange cat might even be the one doing the peeing. To make sure, close off pet doors while you're not home. This can help reduce the stress your cat may have if he's intimidated by intruders.

- Ultrasound or X-rays may find kidney stones that a urine test could miss. Call around for price quotes since this can be expensive.

- If these measures don't work, your cat may need the additional help for declawed cats described below.

**SHOPPING LIST FOR DECLAWED CATS WITH LITTER BOX PROBLEMS**

✓ catnip
✓ different litter brands
✓ Bach Flower Rescue Remedy
✓ Tasha's Herbs for Cats
✓ foods and supplements for stress and immune system (containing C, E and B-complex vitamins)
✓ ascorbic acid (vitamin C), powder or crystals
✓ chicken broth
✓ night light or light timer
✓ Kitty Korner Komber Self-Grooming Aid for CATS

**TRUE STORY**
Owners of declawed cats tell me they maintain the litter box daily. They've tried all different types of litter. A typical complaint from them is that "sometimes he'll be fine for a few weeks, then he'll start up again. . . "

**HELPFUL HINT**
Put a litter box in the bathtub. Many declawed cats would rather scratch at the side of the litter box than on rough litter. Be sure to protect the drain from litter and dust.

## SPECIAL CONSIDERATIONS
### DECLAWED CATS

Declawing makes him "litter-boxed challenged." Because declawed cats have a lower tolerance for stress and a higher risk of pain, their litter box problems frequently are more difficult to solve. Clawed cats aren't nearly so difficult to fix. Even years after the operation, the declawed cat can easily lose bathroom manners when he becomes upset . . . and often, it doesn't take much to upset him.

To minimize the declawed cat's stress levels:

• Give him *daily, supervised* time outdoors. This often relieves his problems for a while.

• Massage him and give him positive attention often.

• Make sure his meals and outdoor times are on a reliable, daily schedule. It's important to minimize changes in routine for a cat who is disabled or may suffer from pain.

• Add vitamins to his diet that can help deal with stress. Vitamins such as B-complex, C (ascorbic acid) and vitamin E each or every other day may help. Squeeze 100 IU vitamin E from a gel cap (made for people or cats) and add a pinch of vitamin C onto their wet food. Some cats may eat the gel straight from a punctured capsule. Anitra Frazier's book *The New Natural Cat* has additional specifics for using vitamins.

• One easy way to give vitamins is to buy multiple vitamins prepared for pets. Many are sold in health food stores. Tasha's Herbs for Cats is one that comes in a variety of formulas. Use the drops as directed. Check the expiration date before buying/using. Avoid products that contain sugar.

• Give him fresh, organic catnip once or twice a week.

• Bad weather and changes in the barometer can affect joints and bones and cause pain in his toes, which may in turn lead to litter box problems. On days when your declawed cat seems especially moody, give him chicken broth with a touch of fresh garlic and a pinch of ascorbic acid (get powder or crystals at a health food store). Put four drops of Bach Flower Rescue Remedy in fresh drinking water. Massages can do wonders on those days. Catnip, too.

- Play peaceful music. Leave a radio on low volume to drown out any distressing noises.

- Put a night light by his litter box.

- When moving to a new house, be especially gentle and conscious of his needs during and after the move. Be slow about letting the declawed cat get full use of the house. (See the Change Happens chapter.)

- Soft laundry is a soft place to pee if you have sore paws. Quilts, crochet afghans and yarn may also entice certain cats. Store these things away from him.

## LITTER BOX CONSIDERATIONS FOR DECLAWED CATS

- Spoon out solids and wet urine spots as often as possible.

- Find out what litter he likes best by trying two or three different litters at a time. Disposable litter boxes or cardboard boxes of litter box size can help with the test. Each week keep one of the brands that he likes, but replace the other boxes with other litter brands. Keep in mind that while clawed cats rarely quit using their customary litter unless something is wrong, declawed cats are more finicky. Sometimes changing the litter will work for a while, but does not address the underlying causes of the litter box problem. Still, it's a worth a try.

- If clay litters haven't worked, try soft litters such as SWHEAT, World's Best Cat Litter, or Cobby Cat. These are biodegradable clumping litters that do not contain sodium bentonite.

⚠ **WARNING**

Do not put compost containing cat waste on the garden. Cat waste is not suitable compost material.

**HELPFUL HINT**

For declawed cats, tilt and shake the litter box to slide nonclumping litter to one end. Some cats with sensitive paws prefer to step onto bare plastic before backing into litter.

- If you're using nonclumping litter, try half the amount you've been using. Shake the litter to one end so only half the floor is covered. Each time you remove the solids, shake to expose half the floor again. He may prefer to step onto a smooth plastic floor.

- Avoid relocating a litter box. If you have to, get a new litter box and set it up in the new location. After he's gotten used to its being there, remove the old one.

## LITTER ALTERNATIVES

If you've tried many types of litter and he doesn't like any of them, here are some more alternatives.

**Grass clippings.** Grass clippings neutralize urine well and are soft. Leave the clippings outside for a few days to let them dry. Protect the floor surrounding the litter box with plain cardboard to avoid grass stains. Monitor the box and remove solids daily. Dump and wash it and add fresh grass as needed. Don't use grass treated with a pesticide or weed killer.

**Newspaper and paper towels.** Line a litter box with a few sheets of newspaper, covered with paper towels. To let cats know it's the litter box, spoon some soiled litter on top of the paper towel. Change the papers after every use.

**Potting soil.** Try using all potting soil or mix some with a non-clumping litter. Gradually keep using more litter and less soil.

## SPECIAL SUPPORT FOR DOUBLE-DECLAWED CATS

If your cat has both front and back claws removed:

- Inspect and clean his ears a few times each year. (See the Home Treatments chapter.)

- Brush and groom him frequently. Help him maintain his coat by letting him roll around on a hard, rough surface. Cats like to groom themselves outside in sunny dirt.

- Scratch his chin and head more often. Rub his face and neck more. Don't massage him in places he doesn't seem to like.

- Install a Kitty Korner Komber Self-Grooming Aid for Cats. This plastic brush attaches to the corner of a wall and can help a double-declawed cat scratch the difficult places. It's found in most pet stores.

## LAST RESORTS

If your cat is not declawed and he's not white, you could keep him outside during the day. (White cats are easily sunburned.) Being outside unsupervised is less safe but has worked as a last resort for many cat owners. If you must keep him outside, try to make your yard as safe as possible by finding a way to keep him inside it, such as by installing a cat kennel or special guards on top of your fence. You can usually find these guards advertised in the back of cat magazines. Because he's more at risk from animals and other dangers at night, bring him indoors and keep him in a confinement room before it gets dark.

One last resort I do not recommend is locking a cat in one room for the rest of its life. Many people tell me "the cat lives in the basement now." This is no way to live with a cat. And no way for a cat to live.

Sometimes nothing works. A cat who continues to pee outside the box is probably suffering. More often, declawed cats are the ones that can't be stopped. Many do suffer. A declawed cat is not likely to get better in a different home with a different family. Although no one likes to bring it up, some cat owners have had no option other than putting a declawed cat to sleep because it's too cruel and dangerous to keep him outside. This decision is never reached lightly. An unchecked urine problem poses a health hazard and can end up costing you a lot of money in home repairs. When suffering is suspected, euthanasia is the most humane alternative.

**TRUE STORY**

I knew a double-declawed cat who was kept on a six-foot chain next to his bed, litter box and food for almost 10 years. And wasn't neutered because he "wasn't let outside." Thank goodness that cat is no longer alive. This was not a good last resort.

**RELATED CHAPTERS**

Just remember—happy, healthy cats don't pee outside the box. Your next cat, if he keeps his claws, has an excellent chance of having good litter box habits for his entire life.

# MISCELLANEOUS PROBLEMS

*Human beings, for one reason or another, may hide their feelings, but a cat does not.*

—ERNEST HEMINGWAY

Does your cat wake you earlier than you want to in the morning? Does he accidentally snag his claws in your clothes? Is he timid? This chapter covers these and other common complaints cat owners have.

## THE EARLY MORNING CAT

A cat who runs across your bed, scratches at your blankets, purrs in your face before you want to get up in the morning, is annoying. The problem gets worse when the owner waits before "giving into" the cat. The cat learns to be obnoxious longer the next morning until the owner gives in again. Pretty soon, the owner is getting up at 3:00 or 4:00 AM. The trick is, don't give him what he wants when he asks you while you're sleeping.

Here are some other things you can do:

- Provide an indoor litter box so he won't pester you to let him outside when he wakes up too early.

- If he's allowed outside, let him out at a regular time, every-day. Don't let him out at any other time of the day. Don't let a cat outside right after you get out of bed. He will learn that bugging you while you're still in bed does not get him what he wants.

- Serve him his meals at regular times each day. Do not feed him as soon as you get out of bed. Take your shower and get your tea ready before giving him his morning meal. He'll get used to it.

**SHOPPING LIST**

- **Morning Cats**
✓ perfume
✓ carpet runner
✓ cat toys

- **Velvet Paw, Screen and Curtain Training**
✓ nail trimmers
✓ nylon netting

- **Sprayer**
✓ urine neutralizer
✓ carpet cleaner
✓ wax paper, carpet runner
✓ organic catnip
✓ vitamins
✓ bare wood post, tree limb or cardboard scratching pad

- **Shy Cats**
✓ cat treats
✓ cat toys

- **Chewers**
✓ fiber supplements
✓ organic catnip
✓ chew toys, pencils, yardsticks

- If the cat likes to cuddle up to your head or neck but you'd rather have him by your feet, gently move him down the bed and pet him. If he moves back up, keep moving him down until he gets tired. Some cats don't like perfume or cologne; spray some on your neck before going to bed.

- Scare him when he hassles you while you're in bed. When he runs across you, lift your knee in front of him and yell "no." Gently shove him off the bed. If he's really bugging me, I sometimes violate my own advice about never holding the cat against his will and will hold and hug him and make it difficult for him to leave. Because cats don't like to be held down, this may curb the behavior faster.

- Protect the carpet by your bedroom door by covering with something sturdy like carpet runner. Cut the carpet runner to match the doorway. As soon as he turns obnoxious, shut him out of the room. The cat won't be happy about being locked out. He will do his best to wear you down by becoming more obnoxious. He'll scratch at the carpet by the door to be let in. Don't give in! If you let him in, he'll be more persistent the next day. If you really have to open your door to make him stop, do not talk to him. Just pick him up and lock him in a room that has a litter box and water and go back to bed.

- Put a scratching post right outside your bedroom door so he'll have a way to vent frustration at not being let in.

- Put toys in other rooms so he can play while you sleep

- Put a cat bed by a window and a bird feeder just outside for him to watch. This helps keep him occupied in the twilight hours when he's most likely to be active.

- Playing with your cat for several minutes, once or twice a day, helps tire him for the night.

## VELVET PAWS

Some cats are sloppy about keeping their claws retracted and will accidentally snag your clothes and furniture and scratch your skin. Teaching a cat to have "velvet paws" means to train the cat not to extend the claws. It also means to teach the owner how to handle the cat so he's never forced to use his claws.

Before beginning, your cat should be used to having his claws trimmed. (See the Hair and Nails chapter.)

*Here is the essence of velvet paw training:* Never let him hurt you. When he does scratch you or snag something, say "ouch!" and trim one or two of his claws. The key to success is to react immediately. Sharply say "ouch!" the instant it happens, even if he snags the clothes you're wearing. Then look at his nails and say, "You need your nails trimmed." Trim one or two claws while talking to him in a gentle tone. Then pull out a lure toy to make him forget about his nail trim, or pet him and tell him he's a good boy. If trying to trim a nail causes fear or panic then wait until the cat is asleep.

### TIPS

• If your cat is frightened while you are holding him, he may extend his claws and try to jump down. Even after he is velvet pawed, he may dig his claws into you when he's suddenly frightened. It's important when holding a cat to always hold him in a such a way and release him in such a way that you avoid his claws touching you. Be ready, willing and able to let him go at any time. Don't hold him so that if he must scramble to get away, he'll hurt you. And never hold him close to your face, because you are unprotected should he bolt.

• While he's learning, avoid handling him while wearing delicate clothing. If he tends to scratch you accidentally, wear long sleeves and handle him very carefully until he's used to keeping his claws in. If your cat's claws are trimmed properly, accidental scratching will not usually break the skin.

- Keep your cat's claws trimmed short all the time. This, in itself, will prevent most accidental snagging. Even the best cat can't prevent a sharp point from catching material and hurting your skin.

## CURTAIN AND SCREEN CLIMBING

Kittens will sometimes climb curtains. Adult cats are usually too heavy for curtains but can rip window screens. It's best to stop this behavior as soon as it starts and get your cat off on good window habits.

Protect your curtains by pinning them up out of the way whenever the kittens are loose. If he tries to jump on the curtains, say "no" immediately and carry him to the scratching post.

If your cat scratches a window screen, spend a few minutes a day with him when the window is open and the screen is exposed. Whenever a claw goes into the screen, deliver a firm "no!" and clip a nail. If he does it again, clip another nail. If he does it a third time, shut the window. Until he stops damaging the screen, keep your windows closed when you aren't around, or cover the open window with nylon netting.

## SPRAYING

When a cat sprays, he's marking territory with a horizontal stream of urine. He stands high up on all fours and aims at the wall. This is a different problem than urinating outside the box. Spraying is considered a behavior problem whereas a urine problem is often a sign of illness. I consider spraying a sign of aggression, low self-esteem or stress which is helped with diet and exercise. In any case, if the problem is not solved, his spray could destroy your house. Although it's less potent and less likely in neutered cats, even some fixed cats still spray.

## CAUSES AND CURES

- If you catch him spraying, firmly tell him "no." Carry him to a room with a litter box and lock him in. Clean and neutralize the soiled area before letting your cat out. If you can, wash the area again while your cat watches. This shows him the walls are yours, not his.

- Tape wax paper on the walls where he has sprayed. Also protect the floor next to the wall with wax paper or plastic carpet runner.

- If you haven't already done so, spay or neuter your cat. This alleviates most spraying problems.

- Make sure you play with him and that he uses the scratching post every day.

- A bare wooden post or tree limb for him to scratch may be help relieve the stress of a cat who sprays. The bare wood simulates a natural place for his paws to leave his scent.

- Provide healthy diet and exercise. (See the chapters on those topics.)

- Give him vitamins and catnip to help ease stress. (See the Litter Box Blues chapter.)

- If the cat lives indoors-only, confine him to one room for a week or two. Then gradually let him have use of the house again. (See the Newcomer chapter.)

- If he goes outside, let him outdoors only at the regular time. Wait at least an hour if he was due to go out soon after a spraying incident. If he has no regular outdoor time, don't let him outside until the next day. If the problem persists, confine him in a room for a week or two. This helps limit the territory he feels he must protect. When you let him back out into the house, see if his spraying has stopped. If it has, you may try outside

**TRUE STORY**

Sam was two years old when I adopted him. He used to raise havoc in the apartment—before I had him neutered.

Some nights he'd pull out the drawer of the bird cage so he could stick his arm into the cage and frighten the parakeets. Other nights he would paw the kitchen cabinets and rattle around in the pots and pans. Then, about a month after I adopted Sam, I saw him back up to the wall and shoot a stream of urine.

I called the veterinarian for an appointment to neuter him. Sam never sprayed inside the house again. He even stopped rattling the pots and pans around in the kitchen at night. We found another home for the birds.

walks again, but only if you can stick with a consistent, daily schedule.

- Living in overcrowded situations can cause stress, frustration and anger, which in turn can lead to spraying. The cat may spray to protect the little territory he feels he owns. You can alleviate overcrowding by taking some cats outside regularly. (See the Outside/Inside chapter.)

- Sometimes a cat sprays after seeing or even hearing a strange cat outside the house. Keeping a scratching post near the windows or doors can help your cat relieve frustration or anger.

- If your cat gets upset by a strange cat, distract him with a lure toy or a food treat *before* he sprays. Say things like, "You are so brave, Lincoln!" He'll probably cool down and forget about being mad.

- Keep a bed by the window so that he can watch and protect the house while he naps. He may feel less threatened if he can see outside. I don't believe that covering the windows is a good idea. You can't hide something from an animal who has even better hearing and smelling capabilities than his eyesight.

- Provide a low, horizontal scratching board. Scratching horizontally is another way a cat will mark territory.

- If you've tried everything and he still sprays, ask your veterinarian to check for impacted anal glands, and for medication which may alleviate the problem. Some cats truly aren't meant to stay indoors and may benefit by a temporary use of tranquilizers. (Also, see the Litter Box Blues chapter.) Outside may be the best alternative.

## SHY CATS

Does your cat run away when other people or cats are around? Is he too easily frightened by everyday events? Although cats have a tendency to run away first before approaching something new, eventually his curiosity should win over. Cats don't hide very much. Some cats will hide for a couple days after a move. Other than that, not many cats hide everyday unless something went wrong.

The stress of being on the streets and in the shelter can cause some cats to go into "shell shock" which can force a cat to hide. And although dogs can make some cats hide a lot, he could be sick so take him to the veterinarian to be sure. Also, being handicapped can cause some shyness. As well as being not handled much, mishandled, mistreated or abused, being ignored and rarely praised or petted, especially when young, can also produce a shy cat. It has been proven that proper handling of kittens leads to healthier cats.

### WHAT ELSE TO DO?

- Gradually accustom your cat to handling and massages. Be sure to stop *before* he gets nervous. (For tips on technique, see the Hands-On Experience chapter.)

- Play with your cat daily, one-on-one, in a bedroom with the door closed. Use lure toys or string, let him catch it often. A 15 minute session each day should help increase confidence and overcome shyness. Don't used large feathers as a toy since they may be intimidating for a timid cat. And remember to always store string or lure toys away from cats when you aren't around.

- Say his name and talk to him gently whenever he comes around, or even just looks in the doorway.

- Encourage him to use the scratching post more. (See the Scratching Posts, Exercise and Play chapters.)

- If he doesn't like being held, avoid picking him up. Pet him where he's standing or lying down. If you want to hold him, get down on his level and gently walk him into your lap to avoid picking him up. He'll be more likely to approach you on his own over time that way.

- If your friends are visiting, warn them not to pick up the shy cat. Ask them not say his name or "it's okay" if your cat runs away or acts scared. Just ignore him unless he approaches you or your friends. Then talk to him gently or get out a lure toy and play.

- Provide him with elevated hiding places or a special cat bed. Cats like to view the world from a high vantage point. Looking down at the family can build trust.

- Train your cat to come when called. This helps built trust. (See the Basic Training chapter.)

- If he's extremely timid, set up a confinement room as described in the Newcomer chapter. A big house is overwhelming for a really scared guy. Keep him in his nursery for one to three weeks. Feed and visit regularly. Use treats to entice him into having contact with you. Spend as much time each day in the room playing with him, massaging him and being with him. The more he responds to your touch, coming towards you and coming to your call, the more freedom he can be allowed.

- I do one thing to a shy cat that I don't otherwise do: If I know it's a time when he won't hurt me, I hold him against his will for a brief second or two—long enough to pet him using a forceful yet compassionate stroke, but not so long that he gets really fussy. Sometimes just a little loving hug can make some cats who were thinking of getting away decide to hang out for a few more seconds. Also, it helps to settle him down a second or two *before* letting him go, so he's likely to hang around longer next time. Don't wait until he's antsy to let a shy cat go.

## CRYING CATS

When your cat cries, he's trying to tell you something. Find out what he wants. Does he want to go outside, or eat, or play? Or is he maybe sick, lonely, frightened?

- If your cat cries while using the litter box, call the veterinarian immediately.

- Ask him, "What do you want Louie?" and follow him to where he walks. A cat will walk to his play, eating or outside area. If it's not the right time to eat or go outside or you can't play right now, tell him "not now." Do NOT give in! Direct a clawed cat to the scratching post. After he's done, he won't remember what he was whining about. If you change your mind later and want to take him outside or give him his special treat, wait until he's sleeping, then call, "Here, Louie" to give it to him.

- Sticking to his daily routine of play, meals and outdoor times helps avoid unnecessary whining. Playing with him at least twice a day can help.

- If he cries to you for something that he is scheduled to get, give it to him as soon as he asks for it. Don't let him cry for half an hour and then give in.

- If he doesn't lead you anywhere, he may just want lots of lovin' from you—that is, petting and massage. Or he may be frightened or not feeling well. Pet him and comfort him. Put a night light on where he sleeps at night. Keep an eye on him and take him to the veterinarian if he shows any symptoms of illness or injury.

- Make sure the cat gets attention during the times when he's quiet and good.

- If these measures don't work, your cat could simply be a natural born whiner, like Louie. He has been since week one.

## CHEWERS

Although it is relatively rare, cats sometimes develop destructive chewing habits on objects such as furniture, electrical cords or shoes. Much of the time, the cat's chewing will be caused by stress, boredom or a nutritional deficiency.

**TRUE STORY**

Louie comes and tells me when he wants certain things. Throughout the day, he'll ask me for playing, food, massages or outside. I give him what he wants only if it's about the usual time he normally gets them. By knowing he can depend on routine, he cries a lot less. On the occasions that I cannot give him what he wants, I tell him, "Not now" and he gives up on it.

**WARNING**

Cover electrical cords with plastic safety coverings from a hardware store. A spray-on repellent may not be enough to stop him chewing.

Because each cat is different, use your instinct to decide what might be causing the problem. In any case, secure your house by covering the electrical cords, putting your shoes away and protecting the things he's likely to chew. To let the cat know that's your property, put perfume on them if you want. To let him know he can chew on them, spray catnip on his stuff.

### HERE, CHEW ON THIS!

At the same time, set up things around the house he is allowed to chew on, such as:

- A yardstick or small branch tucked under a sofa cushion where it can be steady while he chews on it

- A dog chew toy or large soup bone, left in a place where he likes to chew

- A cardboard box; open the top flap of a box about cat-height so he can chew on the lid

- Unsharpened graphite pencils

When you catch him chewing on things he shouldn't, tell him "not here" and direct him to something he can chew. If it's there, he'll go to it. Even then, rather than set your cat up for failure and yourself up for disappointment, don't leave your fancy shoes out. When you leave the house, cover up valuable things he's likely to chewed. Keep the electrical cords covered. Go back to what he was chewing on and protect it or put it away.

Once you think you know what caused the chewing problem, customize your approach as follows:

To minimize stress, establish an exercise regimen as outlined in the Scratching Posts, Exercise and Play and Litter Box Blues chapters. Play with him regularly. Vitamins can lessen stress.

If he's alone for extended periods of time, he may be bored. Consider getting another cat for him to play with. If that's not realistic, see the section on Owning an Only Cat  in the Adoption chapter for suggestions. In addition, increase your time with him.

He may be chewing objects because he's not getting enough fiber. Add pet fiber supplement, cooked brown rice and/or catnip to his diet. Some fiber supplements are made for cats. (See Products and Resources in the appendix for sources of these supplements or catnip.)

**RELATED CHAPTERS**

- *Adoption*
- *Newcomer*
- *Basic Training*
- *Diet*
- *Hands-On Experience*
- *Litter Box Blues*
- *Scratching Posts, Exercise and Play*
- *Outside/Inside*

Sara E. Levine

# Aging

# GROWING OLD AND SAYING GOOD-BYE

*You are supposed to outlive your cat. Saying good-bye is the most difficult thing of all about being a cat owner.*

—ANNIE BRUCE

Time passes very quickly when we own cats. All too soon it will be time to say good-bye. Cats live to be about 15 to 20 years and I keep hearing about older cats all the time. And as the cat matures, age brings on problems similar to people's—such as stiff joints, failing eyesight and hearing.

Signs of aging include reduced mobility, diminished appetite and corresponding weight loss and occasional incontinence. When you first notice one of these symptoms, ask the veterinarian to give him a physical and a blood test.

As the cat ages and has trouble getting around, there are several things you can do:

• Unless otherwise instructed by your veterinarian, feed an older cat three or four very small wet meals a day so he doesn't have to process so much food at once. Stop using low-fat or "senior" food to help him fight against the tendency to lose weight. Don't feed him dry food anymore, it strains the kidneys, which often are the first major organ to quit.

• To keep him fit, keep encouraging the use of the scratching post. Have one by his bed. And take him on short walks outside. But remember that he isn't good at protecting himself now so make sure to supervise him at all times.

• Keep a litter box and water bowl on each level in your home. Asking an elderly person to climb stairs (and relatively tall stairs at that) to use the bathroom is unreasonable. Make toilet provisions on every level for a cat who has trouble getting around.

**SHOPPING LIST**

✓ floor-level, warm bed
✓ extra litter box
✓ whatever he will eat
✓ tuna
✓ baby food (chicken, beef, turkey)
✓ blanket or towel

**OPTIONAL**

✓ burial basket, box
✓ headstone

**CATS ARE LIKE PEOPLE**

When we get old, everything we do is more of a challenge.

**TRUE STORY**

When diagnosed with a kidney problem, our Sam had about a week left.

Every day of that week, I took him into the yard and spent hours watching him while he enjoyed his favorite places and did his favorite things: talking to birds, dozing off, smelling plants, enjoying the sun, making believe he's a great hunter.

I took time to comfort Sam with my hands and told him about how we met and our years together. . . about how much I appreciated his company, how much I loved him and how he was there for me through hard times. I thanked him for sharing his life with me.

Three days before he died, he stopped eating and began drinking a lot of water because his kidneys were shutting down.

It's a difficult thing to plan your own cat's death. But my husband made it easier when he said he "did not want Sam to have any bad days." I realized I felt the same way. The next morning we took Sam into the backyard for a last visit. Then, all too soon, after 14 years of loving and

*continued on the next page*

- Have a night light so he can find the box more easily at night.

- Put a warm, draft-free bed at floor level so he doesn't have to climb or jump to take his nap.

- Gently massage, or simply hold, his frail body when you have the time.

## A CAT'S FINAL DAYS

When your cat's appetite and bladder control are completely gone, if his breathing is difficult, or he drinks constantly, he may be near his end. Check with the veterinarian. Give him whatever he wants. Even "no-no" foods such as tuna or baby food.

As the end nears, you will need to make some horrible decisions. Dying at home in "his own time" is often not without suffering. You may want to consider euthanasia. It's a difficult decision to let go, but sometimes it's more humane to have a compassionate veterinarian put him to sleep.

If you decide to have him put to sleep, make arrangements with the veterinarian. Many veterinarians will come to your house or you can bring your cat there. While you're on the phone, discuss with the doctor what to do with the body. You can bury it, arrange to have it cremated, or let them take care of the remains. Ask any questions now, especially delicate ones, because you won't be in the mood to ask about them later.

When it's time to go, take a blanket or towel with you so your cat can die on a soft bed rather than a hard table. Have someone else drive so that you can hold your cat in your lap. He's so sick that he doesn't need a carrier unless you are driving alone. And, you won't have to drive home by yourself.

The veterinarian will ask you to sign a release form before starting. Ask him to not scruff your cat at anytime. Let his last moments be as dignified as possible. Put the blanket under your cat on the table and spend some tender moments with him.

When you are ready to have him put to sleep, the veterinarian might need to shave your cat's leg so that he can see the correct vein in which to make the injection. It's okay if you leave before the actual euthanasia shot. Or you can stay. It won't be easy either way. Go with whatever you think you can handle. Don't feel guilty later for not "being there"—your cat knows you love him.

## HANDLING THE GRIEF

It's okay to grieve the loss of your cat. Take all the time you need. It's very difficult to lose a companion you live with, even if he's not human. Many people don't realize how badly they feel until the cat is truly gone. Don't feel too bad when others don't understand your grief—to many people, it was "just a cat." If you are easily hurt by a lack of compassion, tell them that you lost a "close friend of the family" and leave it at that.

Some cat owners hold a memorial ceremony to help deal with the loss and establish closure. Some write good-bye letters and bury the letters with his remains along with his favorite toy. Others add a grave marker to identify his grave. Do whatever seems right to you.

Your local shelter may offer a support group where you can talk about your loss. You may also want to take some stress vitamins, exercise, relax in soothing hot baths and eat as healthfully as possible so you don't react to his death by getting sick.

When the time is right, think about getting another cat. It is very healing to get another cat. Although many people may think they are "paying a tribute to old Simon" by waiting to adopt, what about the new "Fred" that's waiting in the shelter for you today? He could be ashes by tomorrow. *Cats need you.* Give another cat a chance in your home. "Simon would have wanted it that way."

*continued from the previous page*

living with Sam, it was time to let him go.

When the veterinarian told us he would shave Sam's inner thigh and inject the lethal shot there, I ran crying from the room—I couldn't watch him die.

Sam died in his "father's" arms. Bruce said it was very quick and then Sam was gone. Afterwards, Bruce came out into the waiting room and cried with me.

We had Sam cremated. When we got his ashes back, we held a ceremony with candles, a song and eulogies, and buried his ashes in a small wicker basket. He rests now in his favorite "rolling around" place, at the base of a pine tree.

### ⚠ BUYER'S REMORSE

Don't adopt a new cat just because he *looks* like good ol' Simon did—there is *no way* he'll be like your old cat. Each cat is different. Look at his behavior, not his looks. Read the Adoption chapter.

It's very easy to bring home the wrong cat shortly after losing one. To help avoid this, volunteer with your local shelter to be a foster home for a few months. If you're unsure about what to foster, ask for black male cats. Adopt the cat you love to live with!

Sara E. Levine

# Appendix

# DECLAWING DRAWBACKS

*I wouldn't declaw a cat if you*
*paid me $1,000 per nail!*

—DR. LOUIS J. CAMUTI, D.V.M.
(A PRACTICING VETERINARIAN OF 58 YEARS)

Declawing is presented to cat owners as a rational choice yet it is a very expensive venture. Owning a declawed cat is definitely not cheap. We choose it because we've been convinced it will solve a problem. Yet declawing causes so many problems. Peeing outside the box is just one, which is enough. Cat urine can destroy your home much faster and more thoroughly than claws. *Declawed cats are definitely litter box challenged.* Declawed cat owners call me almost always about litter box problems. They were not warned of the declawing drawbacks.

Declawing immediately jeopardizes the cats' entire life in many, many ways. Besides challenging the physical and mental capabilities of the cat, many people can't and won't face the stench. Many will get rid of the cat, not knowing that declawing was what started their mess. Others will have him euthanized. Or he'll be imprisoned in one room or forced to live outside. Many declawed cats are abandoned. When he's outside, he is an easy target for predators.

Even if he stays indoors, he won't have much of a life. He won't be able to use carpeted cat trees like clawed cats. He'll be clumsy, more prone to infections, more moody and more trouble than a clawed cat.

Clawed cats take virtually no time or effort to learning how to use a scratching post. Dealing with urine problems from a cat who cannot learn to use a litter box requires the patience of a saint.

## DID YOU KNOW?

In Australia, Austria, Belgium, Brazil, Denmark, Finland, Germany, Netherlands, New Zealand, Norway, Portugal, Spain, Sweden, Switzerland, and the United Kingdom (Britain)—*declawing is illegal or considered inhumane*. The list keeps growing.

Those opposed to declawing include the British Veterinary Association, the Royal College of Veterinary Surgeons, the American Society for the Prevention of Cruelty to Animals, the Humane Society of the United States, The Association of Veterinarians for Animal Rights, the Cat Fanciers Association and the People for the Ethical Treatment of Animals.

Dr. Kimberly Harrison, D.V.M. at The Cat Doctor in Aurora, Colorado, collected data on cats with litter box problems that were not medically related: About 90 percent were declawed cats.

Both Lisa Booker, director of Every Creature Counts in Lyons, Colorado, and Audrey Boag, director of Alley Cat Allies in Indian Hills, Colorado, agree that 90 percent of the cats with litter box problems are declawed. Other shelters have reported similar findings.

## DID YOU KNOW?

Declawing is the removal of bones, tendons, ligaments and claws to the first knuckle of each toe.

Declawing undermines the health, and consequently, the behavior of the cat.

Declawing can lead to worse problems.

Declawing has only started in about the last 30 years. Clawed cats have been living indoors much longer than that.

### TRUE STORY

I knew one woman who spent $800 to have her cat's feet fixed. Loose bones caused some claws to become infected. A couple even tried to grow back. This bill cost more than the price of her sofa and bed, both damaged by cat urine.

## CATS ARE LIKE PEOPLE

You don't have to declaw a cat because all your other cats are declawed. Cats, like people, recognize immediately when a fellow cat is handicapped. It's okay to mix clawed and declawed cats inside the house.

And few of us, when it comes down to it, are saints. How would you feel if your couch was *totally* ruined by urine? At least with claw destruction, you can have it recovered. Or your carpet, pad and floorboard stink to the point that they have to be replaced? I know owners of declawed cats who have had to do this. People who own clawed cats rarely call me about extensive damage such as this.

A cat needs his claws to groom, scratch, climb, "knead" and to rake cat litter in comfort. Adopting a declawed cat is different than adopting one who has all his fingers. Don't expect him to be the same, feel the same, act the same, cost the same, and be as healthy as able-bodied cats.

Not every declawed cat develops litter box problems but many do. "I did what my vet said. . . . Our home is still being destroyed by cat urine. . . .We've replaced the carpet. . . .We threw out the sofa. . . We clean the litter daily. . . .I'm thinking of getting rid of him." These calls come from declawed cat owners. From what I've seen, it takes very little to get a declawed cat to start peeing.

Cats exercise differently from dogs: Cats stalk, dogs hunt. Cats evolved to sleep and scratch, not run and pant. Cats are not aerobic creatures. It's very difficult to get a cat to run at all, let alone on sore feet. Some declawed cats have sore feet their entire lives (not just the two weeks some veterinarians may claim). Every cat scratches, whether Mommy taught him to or not. Declawing does not change the cats' internal need to do these things. It does, however, make it more painful and challenging.

*Mayo Clinic Family Health Book*, David E. Larson, MD, editor in chief, 1996, illustrates how some people are affected by amputation:

"The surgical removal of a body part also can be an emotionally demanding event. There may be pain in the stump or the sensation, sometimes painful, that the limb or part of the limb is still present, so called phantom limb pain. In addition, your self image, *self confidence* and self worth may be affected. . . . In addition to drawing on the body's healing capacity, an amputation also requires a *significant psychological adjustment . . .*" [emphasis added].

Confidence *is* diminished in the declawed cat. Many cat owners report that their cat's personality changed drastically after being declawed. Many cat owners are disappointed, most tell me they would never have it done again.

Some argue that removing the front claws is of no consequence since a cat "fights" primarily "with his hind paws." This is not the whole truth: A cat *escapes* by climbing trees with his front claws. Which would be better? A cat who has defenses only to fight, or one who can also get away? Too many declawed cats are rushed to emergency rooms after trying to get away from dogs. Contrary to myth, most cats don't like to fight. Cats would rather get away.

Many people respond to litter box problems by letting the cat outside. When outside stops "working" and the doctor's advice fails, and if the cat continues to pee inside the house, the cat will be given new "last resorts." Alternatives will be used that the veterinarian didn't mention at the time of declawing. Now without claws, he's likely to be squirted, spanked, locked outside, or locked inside in the basement, abandoned, given away or destroyed. Not many cat owners will let a cat destroy an entire house. Many cat owners are unconsciously made aware that declawing is nowhere near the "last resort." Death is.

## STILL CONSIDERING DECLAWING?

If you really think declawing will save you time and money, before signing up for the operation, ask the veterinarian:

- Will he guarantee your declawed cat won't start peeing? Will he pay for the urine tests, neutralizers, or damage?

**DID YOU KNOW?**

The declawing procedure involves anesthesia and cutting off the cat's toes to the first knuckle. Many veterinarians use something similar to pruning shears. Others use a "fine scalpel" technique, or laser. They claim these are cleaner procedures—which they probably are—but declawing no matter how you cut it, is crippling the cat.

The operation takes about 10 minutes and can cost anywhere from $40 to $250. But the costs and pain don't stop there. For some cats and owners, the problems are just beginning.

If the cat comes does with an infection or develops behavioral problems as a result of declawing, the follow-up care and repairs can be very expensive.

**DID YOU KNOW?**

If a veterinarian says he has a study that says declawing has no side effects, scrutinize the validity of the data: Over what time frame was the study taken? Was data collected 5, 10, 20 *years* later? What age groups were studied? Were injuries, illness, diseases and behavior problems such as litter box problems recorded?

**IF YOUR VETERINARIAN DECLAWS, HAVE AVAR SEND YOUR VET INFORMATION ON DECLAWING. CALL OR WRITE:**

AVAR (The Association of Veterinarians for Animal Rights)
PO Box 208
Davis, CA 95617-0208

(916) 759-8106
(916) 759-8116 fax
http://arrs.envirolink.org/avar

Will he guarantee your cat's personality won't change? Or that he won't become a biter?

- Is there risk of infection, a second operation or diabetes? How much will that cost? (Sometimes pieces of loose bone can cause infection, requiring subsequent operations.)

- How will you exercise a declawed cat? How much time was spent in veterinarian school discussing ways to exercise cats? Were considerations taken in account for being handicapped?

- How many declawed cats has he euthanized for a litter box problem?

- If your cat is being declawed because the veterinarian claims it will make him less "dangerous," ask how dangerous it could be if he pees all over the place. Declawing will not make a cat less dangerous. Besides, if the cat is so "dangerous" that surgery is necessary, remember that there are millions of cats being euthanized every year due to lack of homes who are not dangerous and won't require expensive surgery.

## DECLAWING ISN'T THE ONLY BAD IDEA

- A tendonectomy is a relatively new surgical procedure that severs the tendon in each toe. The cat will not be able to control or extend his claws. You will still have to trim his claws. He'll be unable to perform his much-needed scratching, pulling and tugging exercise. He could face years with painful feet and bear the same litter box or biting problems as his amputee brothers. *Do not choose this option.* It has the same disabling impact on exercise as declawing does. Even though no amputation takes place, tendons are very painful when torn or cut. In people a torn tendon in the foot can take years to heal.

- Avoid adopting a declawed cat. If you are so afraid of claws, a cat, as well as dogs, birds and many other pets, are not for you.

## MOSES' STORY

While writing this book, I had to have one of my own cats put to sleep. Moses was a beautiful black and white, declawed cat.

He was picked up as a stray and taken to a shelter. On the fifth day he was scheduled for euthanasia. Minutes before being destroyed he was rescued by a local shelter volunteer. I took him in as a foster cat. He had wrinkled pads on his mutilated feet.

He wasn't suitable for adoption. He peed in the bathroom sink and a couple of other spots that were not a litter box. He would bite my hands at the slightest movement. He was easily stressed and quick to hiss. He whined when he scratched. He pawed at the area around his box longer than his buddies.

Many things were different about him. And I could tell he had been abused, he paid such close attention to hands and squirt bottles.

It took several months to get his biting under control. For his peeing problem I took him to a few different doctors for urine tests and examinations. I talked with a behaviorist.

After many suggestions, he was still misbehaving. I started thinking how amputee humans deal with their pain and stress. And I applied similar techniques on Moses. My special regime, detailed in the Litter Box Blues chapter, kept his peeing problem at bay for about two years.

Then his peeing became more frequent and less isolated to certain spots. He peed in my dresser, on my desk, in the bed, even on my husband's neck once while he slept. Some days were worse than others. He appeared to want attention but a closer look told me Moses was in pain. It kept getting worse. I took him to another veterinarian. Then he started peeing on carpet, that's when I knew it was time to have him put out of his misery. Moses was peacefully put to sleep.

### DID YOU KNOW?

Litter box problems are practically the only calls I get from declawed cat owners. Clawed cat owners call me for a wide variety of reasons.

Most declawed cat owners report litter box problems beginning at earlier ages, usually before the age of eight.

Clawed cat litter box problems typically begin later in life and are usually prompted by a medical condition.

If Moses had his claws, he could have lived outside. I do not believe declawed cats should be kept or left outside unsupervised. I also don't believe it's healthy or safe to live with cat urine problems inside the house. And I did not want to return a peeing cat a shelter, all of which are burdened enough with *good* cats. Besides, he might get a home with people who would abandon him (which may be how he lost his first home). I believe he was suffering. I loved him way too much for the options left to him.

I named him Moses because declawing makes a cat a slave to his disability as well as making the cat owner a slave to the disabled cat. In the end, it's the owner who becomes slave to the litter box, to the biting, to illness—burdened with chores and bills that should never have been.

I wanted Moses here with me when this book came out to show you just how smart he was. I taught him tricks in just a few lessons. He came running when I called for him. Moses wasn't an attack cat. Declawing didn't save his life. It probably caused his litter box problems. It limited his and my options and paved the way for his abandonment and his death.

My tribute to Moses was to find another cat who needed a home. The day after Moses died and with swollen eyes from crying, I went to a shelter in Denver and found a big, black and white three-year-old. He gets along just fine with my other three adult cats. He has beautiful, whole feet and is smart, as most cats are.

I named my new cat Abraham Lincoln in hopes that American cats will be free someday: free from the option of being permanently disabled; and cat owners free from unnecessary bills and work. Cats never used to need antidepressants or fancy litters. Cats didn't used to pee outside the box until they got sick or old—then declawing came along.

Moses was three and a half years old.

# CUTE CAT TRICKS

*Cats virtually always underestimate human intelligence just as we, perhaps, underestimate theirs.*
—ROGER CARAS

I have mixed emotions about tricks . . . I don't really approve of them for cats. One reason is because professionally trained tricksters must be kept hungry to perform. Also, I think that teaching an animal to do tricks compromises their dignity, especially a cat.

But everyone loved it when my Moses did tricks. He learned them in a day or two and became a polished performer after about a month of one-minute lessons. "If I can teach Moses to do these, how difficult is it to get a cat to use the scratching post?"

## THE "WHAT IT IS" TRICK

Also known as the "give me five" or "shake hands" trick.

1. Find a place to train your cat that is up off the floor, such as a table top. Having the cat higher up is easier on the trainer and puts the cat into a training "mode" as well.

2. Wait until your cat is hungry, such as before his regularly scheduled wet meal.

3. Have a few special food treats he likes but doesn't normally get at hand.

4. Call your cat to come for his meal and give a small treat when he arrives.

5. Put the second treat in your right hand.

6. Say, "Moses, what it is?" Hold your right hand out but slightly away from him so that he has to use his paw to reach the food. When his paw touches or gets close to your right hand, give him the treat.

**SHOPPING LIST**

✓ very special food treat

**RECOMMENDED READING**

✓ Show Biz Tricks for Cats, by Anne Gordon with Steve Duno, 1996.

**HELPFUL HINTS**

Not every cat will perform tricks, but if you have a cat that likes food, the outdoors or playing, then he'll probably be able to learn one trick or another.

A cat who has a tendency to use her paws, mouth or voice is likely to learn tricks that use those parts. Make up your own tricks. But avoid teaching a cat to "sit." It's boring and beneath them.

7. Repeat until your cat begins to touch your hand regularly. After the third day, don't give him a treat if he just comes close.

8. Once he begins touching your right hand, put the treat in your left hand but still have your cat touch your right hand. Don't give him any treat unless he touches your right hand.

9. Start requiring him to always use the same paw (left or right) to shake hands with.

10. Occasionally, make your cat perform the command without food and just before he is allowed outside.

11. Try to end the training session on a well-performed command. Don't wait until he's bored or tired. And don't expect your cat to perform the same trick more than 10 times in a row. For that reason, keep the training sessions under 60 seconds, one to three times a day.

## THE "GIMMIE SOME" COMMAND

Also known as the "kiss me" trick, Moses would reach his little face up to mine and it was so cute!

1. Only do this with a cat that won't claw or bite your cheek to get to some food. Follow the same procedure as above but wait for him to sniff your face before giving him the treat. Try using a bit of baby food smeared on your cheek. The closer he gets to your cheek, the sooner he should get his treat.

2. Once he's been successful, don't settle for less. Always require him to touch you in a certain place to get his treat.

3. As time goes on, make him reach farther to kiss you.

# CAT MAINTENANCE SCHEDULE

## ADOPTION

spay/neuter—do NOT declaw
leukemia test
veterinarian examination
distemper shot
rabies shot
trim claws
vitamins

## DAILY

talk to/say name/praise
encourage use of scratching post
feed wet food
fresh water
play and/or walk outside
touch/pet
brush daily if needed
lift solids and shake litter box—more frequently for a
    declawed cat
massage declawed cat

## WEEKLY

dump and fill box with new litter—more frequently for old
    or sick cat, declawed cats or multiple-cat households
check condition of litter box area
feed organic catnip—once a week;  twice or more weekly
    for a declawed cat
brush weekly during shedding season
hairball remedy

## MONTHLY

trim nails

wash box—more often for a declawed cat

brush

buy cat food and litter

wash water bowl

## YEARLY

veterinarian examination

inspect and clean ears—more often for double declawed cat

inspect teeth for brown tartar

note sleeping, eating, drinking and litter box habits

## AS NEEDED (THESE THINGS USUALLY LAST YEARS)

vaccines  (see note below)

new cat toys

new cat beds

recover old tree or buy new cat tree and scratching post

## YEARLY HOLIDAYS

Cats are in special danger during the holidays and should be kept inside on these days:

- October 30 and 31 (Devil's Night and Halloween)
- December 31, January 1 (New Year's Eve and Day)
- Cinco de Mayo (5th of May, Mexican Independence Day)
- July 4 (Fourth of July)
- Any other holiday where firecrackers or gunshots can scare or confuse the cat to run in the wrong direction and get lost by being disoriented

## NOTE: MY PERSONAL BELIEF ABOUT VACCINES

Many holistic veterinarians feel pets are being over-vaccinated. I agree. Without definitive research, however, these are only personal beliefs. Decide what you want for your cat. Keep in mind your local laws and community responsibilities, and what you think is best.

- Keep rabies vaccinations current
- After the initial distemper shots, only revaccinate at age 10
- Avoid feline leukemia shots. The vaccine offers no guarantees so why spend the money?
- Don't vaccinate a cat over the age of 12 if at all possible
- Don't vaccinate a sick or nursing cat
- A cat should be healthy and fully recovered from surgery before getting vaccinated

# CAT ADVOCACY

*The greatness of a nation and its moral progress can be
judged by the way its animals are treated.*

—MAHATMA GANDHI

If you'd like to help cats in general, cats need your help.
There are many ways you can help.

## ANIMAL SHELTERS

Hundreds of animal shelters across the country could use volunteer help as well as donations. Ask what volunteer positions
they have or specific areas you're interested in working with.
Many shelters have a wide variety of volunteer needs, these are
just a few:

- Foster cats in your home

- Write newsletters, stuff envelopes, make phone calls

- Walk and handle caged cats, clean kennels

- Manage the front desk

- Take cats or dogs to visit patients in nursing homes

If you don't have the time to volunteer, cat shelters appreciate donations of cat food, money, books, litter boxes, rubbing
alcohol, heating pads, towels and all sorts of stuff. Some shelters also have thrift stores or rummage sales to raise money,
and welcome your sellable cast-offs.

## HELP KEEP CATS OUT OF LABORATORIES

In the book, *Why Animal Experiments Must Stop*, Vernon
Coleman estimates that worldwide 100,000 to 125,000 animals are used in experiments every hour. In the U.S., according to Coleman, an animal dies every three seconds in laboratories. Many will be cats. In reality, this figure may be conserv-
ative since some laboratories are secretive about their efforts.

The conditions are unbearable, with cats confined to cages so small they can't stand or stretch. Many experiments are conducted without pain killers or anesthesia. You can help discourage such practices.

- Buy products that aren't tested on animals. There are many companies that won't use animals to test their cosmetics or household cleaners.

- Write your senator or state representative concerning lab animal issues.

- Get your cat tattooed and urge others to do so. It's a federal offense for a laboratory to accept or test on tattooed animals (See Products and Resources in the appendix.)

For more information on what you can do to save animals from inhumane testing procedures contact:

The American Anti-Vivisection Society (AAVS)
  801 Old York Road #204
  Jenkintown, PA 19046-1685 USA
  Phone: 215-887-0816

Society for Animal Protection Legislation (SAPL)
  P.O. Box 3719
  Georgetown Station
  Washington, DC 20007
  Phone: 202-337-2334

Animal Welfare Institute (AWI)
  P.O. BOX 3650
  Washington, DC 20007
  Phone: 202-337-2332
  Fax: 202-338-9478
  http://www.animalwelfare.com

## READ ABOUT CAT-RELATED ISSUES

I suggest the following books as rich sources of information:

- *Sixty Seven Ways to Save the Animals,* by Anna Sequoia

with Animal Rights International, 1990.

- *Why Animal Experiments Must Stop*, by Vernon Coleman, 1991.

- *Slaughter of the Innocent,* by Hans Ruesch, 1983.

*The Animals' Agenda* is a bimonthly magazine that informs people about animals rights and cruelty-free living for the purpose of inspiring action for animals. Call or write:

The Animals' Agenda
1301 S. Baylis Street, Suite 325, PO Box 25881
Baltimore, MD 21224
Phone: 410-675-4566
Fax: 410-675-0066
World Wide Web: www.animalsagenda.org

## HELP STOP DECLAWING

Declawing is a disabling procedure performed on cats by veterinarians, mostly in the United States. Declawing is unnecessary. It is illegal or considered inhumane in several countries.

- Ask your veterinarian to stop declawing all cats.

- Patronize veterinarians who refuse to declaw.

- Have AVAR send information to veterinarians who continue to declaw.

The Association of Veterinarians for Animal Rights (AVAR)
P.O. Box 208
Davis, CA 95617-0208
Phone: 916-759-8106
http://arrs.envirolink.org/avar

## HELP OTHER CAT OWNERS

The more you learn about cat behavior, the more you can help others improve the relationship they have with their cats.

- Talk with other cat owners. You can get into cat discussion groups on the Internet.

- Wear cat clothes around town and when people ask about your cats, you can tell them what you know.

## HELP FERAL CATS

"Feral" means "wild." Feral cats either grew up wild or turned wild after being lost or abandoned. They live in feral "colonies" with other wild cats. Sometimes a person or a group will act as a "caretaker" for a colony. Caretakers provide food and water and occasionally a small shelter, and spaying or neutering of the entire colony. Cared-for ferals can live as long as 10 years; without a caretaker, about two years. As long as they aren't breeding and are left alone they pose no threat to humans.

A feral cat is hardly ever suitable for adoption as a pet. Some owners have had success retraining feral cats, but it took years. Some semiferals are able to adjust if caught soon enough. It's best to let ferals live with their own kind. Ferals do not need your home. Ferals *are* at home in the wild.

### WHY BE CONCERNED ABOUT FERAL CATS?

If feral cats continue to breed and multiply, their numbers "swell quickly to unmanageable magnitude," according to Esther Mechler, director of Spay/USA in New York. That's no lie: One pair of cats can produce 420,000 cats in seven years. This problem becomes everyone's responsibility. Without the tireless efforts of volunteers and veterinarians who trap and alter cats, our cities would continue to get overrun with cats.

Destroying feral cats only keeps a steady stream of new cats invading the area. However, if an entire colony is trapped, altered and returned to the same area, their numbers remain steady. Some cities/counties pledge funds to control the population—a form of "animal control." The results have paid off. Studies across the U.S. and Europe have shown not only that the stray cat population is decreasing, but that it is actually cheaper to spay, neuter and return ferals than it is to kill them.

## WHAT TO DO IF YOU FIND A FERAL CAT COLONY

A few shelters may know the location of feral colonies and caretakers in your area. Because some agencies simply kill feral cats and others offer assistance, call different shelters. Ask about organizations whose mission is to spay and neuter feral cats. Some shelters will trap, alter and return the colony *if* the caller or community can locate a caretaker who will commit to feeding and watering the colony every day. Backup caretakers are also needed. Shelters don't like to return fixed ferals to an area that has no steady food and water supply because the cats won't live long under those conditions.

SPAY/USA and Alley Cat Allies has a growing friends of feral felines national network. They can help you organize your community.

## SETTING UP YOUR OWN SPAY/NEUTERING OF FERALS

If you cannot locate a shelter that will fund the operation, collect donations in the neighborhood and then pay a low-cost clinic to do the procedures. Your local shelter might provide the traps if you leave a refundable deposit. This takes serious dedication and commitment, and is doable.

A book called *Feral Friends, A Guide for Living With Feral Cats*, by Audrey Boag, describes how to trap, tame ferals, plus a lot of other information in a small booklet you can order by sending $4.00 to:

Audrey Boag
P.O. Box 714
Conifer, CO 80433

## WHAT ELSE YOU CAN DO FOR FERALS

Raise community awareness. Ferals are easy targets on which to vent abuse.

- Be a big sister or big brother. Set a good example for kids. Let them know that anyone who tortures cats or other animals needs a mental health professional.

- Volunteer to feed and water a cat colony. You must be able to go to the colony every day and have a backup for any day you cannot make it.

- Volunteer to trap ferals and transport them to the vet's office to be altered. Then transport them back to the colony.

- If you see a cat roaming the neighborhood who doesn't appear to be taken care of, consider calling the shelter to have him rescued. Some people will have a stray altered and find him another home. Neighborhood cats are no longer anyone's pet. They don't have regular proper care and they are *not yet* feral. When caught and fixed soon enough in life, a neighborhood stray is quite adoptable. But if he run the streets with little to no human contact, he will lose trust and become feral in no time.

## FERAL CONTACT LIST FOR SPAY AND NEUTERING SERVICES

For information on veterinarians closest to you offering affordable spay and neutering services, contact:

SPAY/USA
750 Port Washington Blvd., Suite B
Port Washington, NY 11050
1-800 248-SPAY (7729), Monday - Friday 9am-4pm

Alley Cat Allies
P. O. Box 397
Mount Rainier, MD 20712
202-667-3630

**ABOUT FERAL CATS**

- Never touch or handle a feral cat.
- Feral cats usually make bad house pets. Ferals live in and prefer the outdoors. They do not consider your home a paradise—to them, it's a prison.
- There are about 60 million feral cats in the U.S. alone. About 17.5 million Americans feed feral cats.
- If a feral is returned to a different colony, he may try to return "home" even if it takes crossing several miles of highways to do it.

# DONATIONS NEEDED

*The cat does not offer services. The cat offers itself. Of course he wants care and shelter. You don't buy love for nothing. Like all pure creatures, cats are practical.*

—WILLIAM S. BURROUGHS

## *I LIKE TOO MANY ORGANIZATIONS TO LIST, BUT SOME OF MY FAVORITES ARE:*

### ✓ SPAY/USA

The mission of Spay/USA is to end pet overpopulation. Spay/USA is a network of volunteers and veterinarians working together to popularize and facilitate spay/neuter services through a nationwide toll-free referral service. Please send donations to:

SPAY/USA
750 Port Washington Blvd., Suite B
Port Washington, NY 11050
1-800-248-SPAY (248-7729)

### ✓ ANIMAL RESCUE & ADOPTION SOCIETY

ARAS is a no-kill shelter for cats and kittens and is dedicated to the prevention of cruelty to animals.
Animal Rescue & Adoption Society
2390 S. Delaware Street
Denver, CO 80223
303-744-6076

### ✓ COLORADO HUMANE SOCIETY

The Colorado Humane Society is another favorite shelter of mine. Send donations to:
Colorado Humane Society
2760 S. Platte River Drive
Englewood, CO 80110
303-781-9344

## ✓ HUMANE SOCIETY OF BOULDER VALLEY

The Humane Society of Boulder Valley is the humane society
in my area.  Find one in your area. I make donations to:

Humane Society of Boulder Valley

2323 55th Street

Boulder, CO  80301

303-442-4030

## ✓ EVERY CREATURE COUNTS

Every Creature Counts is a no-kill shelter who offer spay and
neuter services for feral colonies, low-cost spay and neuter
services for companion pets. Donations can be sent to:

Every Creature Counts

PO Box 1683

Lyons, CO  80540

## ✓ AMERICAN ANTI-VIVISECTION SOCIETY

AAVS provides education involving the use of laboratory animals.  Please send donations to:

American Anti-Vivisection Society (AAVS)

801 Old York Road #204

Jenkintown, PA   19046-1685

215-887-0816

## ✓ ALLEY CAT ALLIES

Alley Cat Allies operates a network that links individuals
together and helps educate the public on the humane techniques available for feral cat colonies.

Alley Cat Allies

P. O. Box 397

Mount Rainier, MD 20712

202-667-3630

# PRODUCTS AND RESOURCES

I buy a lot of cat stuff and get help from a lot of resources. There's no room to list them all. Here are some of my favorites. Most companies will send you a free catalog or information. (For more on cat foods, cat litters and urine neutralizers, local stores and services, see below.)

| THINGS I BUY | WHERE I BUY THEM |
|---|---|
| Felix Katnip Trees & Board<br>    These are covered with sisal fabric and are favorites for my cats. | The Felix Company<br>3623 Fremont Ave. N<br>Seattle WA 98103<br>206-547-0042 |
| Tattoos and register number (see the Tattooing notes after this chart) | TATOO-A-PET<br>6571 SW. 20th Ct.<br>Ft. Lauderdale, FL 33317<br>1-800-TATTOOS (828-8667) |
| Mail order cat supplies, kitty oats, toys, organic catnip | Cats Claws<br>    1-800-783-0977 |
| Pet supplies, natural medicines, vitamins, fiber and food supplements | Pet Sage - Natural medicines, alternative therapies<br>1-800-PET-HLTH (738-4584) |
| European-Style Pet Food Mix for Cats (a grains mix you add to homemade, canned food or plain yogurt) | Sojourner Farms<br>    1-888-TO-SOJOS (867-6567) (toll free) |
| Mail order pet supplies, toys | Drs. Foster & Smith<br>    1-800-826-7206 |
| Vitamins for cats (Tasha's Herbs for cats come in wide variety of formulas) | health food stores<br>    Tasha's Herbs for Cats,<br>    Coyote Springs Co.,<br>    PO Box 9888, Jackson, WY 83002<br>    307-734-0142 |

| THINGS I BUY | WHERE I BUY THEM |
|---|---|
| Chinese herbs for cats | Healing Herbs for Pets (satisfaction guaranteed) 1-888-775-PETS (775-7387) (toll free) |
| Pet food, herbal remedies, pet supplies, vitamins, fiber and food supplements | Whiskers - Holistic Products for Pets 1-800-WHISKERS (944-7537) http://choicemall.com/whiskers |
| Bach Flower Rescue Remedy | health food stores |
| Cardboard scratching pad | The Cat Doctor Dr. Kimberly S. Harrison, DVM 1710 S. Buckley Road Aurora, CO 80017 303-696-7901 |
| Great gifts for cat lovers (clothes, jewelry, knickknacks, Odor Eliminator - reusable bags of neutralizer, and lots more) | Cat, Cats & More Cats P O Box 270 Monroe, NY 10950 1-800-708-CATS (708-2287) www.catscats.com |
| Green Herb carries natural herbs for humans and pets. | Green Herb, LLC 4990 Kipling, Suite 5 Wheat Ridge, CO 80033 Denver Metro Area 303-421-9900 1-888-765-HERB (765-4372) (toll free) |
| Cat trees, carrier cases, catnip herb or pump spray, cat toys, cat food, hairball remedies, combs, brushes, collars, black light, etc. | pet stores; mail order; animal shelters; grocery stores; discount stores; hardware stores |
| Heavy fabric or plastic to protect sofa; crochet hook to repair snags | fabric store |
| Twist upholster pins to attach protection to sofa | hardware store |
| Cat litter (see special section in this appendix) | grocery stores, pet stores |
| Neutralizer for cat urine (see special section below) | hardware stores; pet stores |
| Catalog of dog and cat books | Dog & Cat Book Catalog www.dogandcatbooks.com 1-800-776-2665 |

| THINGS I BUY | WHERE I BUY THEM |
|---|---|
| Convincing pet drivers license with your cat's picture and statistics; comes in different U.S. driver's state licenses. These makes great gifts! Cat owners get a kick out 'em! | Chloe Cards<br>  1118 13th St. Dept 25-B<br>  Boulder, CO 80302<br>  www.chloecards.com<br>  In CO 303-442-7790<br>  1-888-245-6388 (toll free) |
| Cat litter and accessories | see below and the Litter Boxes Etc. chapter |
| Carpet cleaner for cat vomit | vacuum stores; carpet cleaning people |
| Digital thermometer; and a roll of nonskid rubber mat, useful for keeping things on shelves that cat normally knock off | drug stores or discount stores |

## TATTOOING

It is a federal offense for a laboratory to accept or test a tattooed animal. More than 2 million dogs and cats are stolen each year and sold to labs. With a *registered* tattoo, half of tattooed cats and nearly all tattooed dogs are recovered when lost. The tattoo takes just minutes and lasts forever.

### HOW TO GET IT DONE

1. Tatoo-A-Pet is a well-known pet tattoo registry. Call Tatoo-A-Pet at 1-800-TATTOOS (828-8667) and ask for the phone numbers of the tattoo agent closest to you.

2. Make an appointment with the tattoo agent.

3. Get a tranquilizer pill from the vet. Ask how soon before the tattoo to administer it. You may not need to sedate your cat but it's good to be prepared.

4. Take a large beach towel and pillow case to restrain the cat while he's being tattooed. You will probably need to assist the tattoo agent during the procedure since two people are usually needed to steady a cat that is not heavily sedated.

5. Have a cat tattooed in his ear unless he's a show cat. To be extra cautious you can also tattoo him on his on his inner thigh because some cats have shown up for sale to laboratories with their ear cut off. (Dogs are usually tattooed on the inner thigh where there is little hair.) The tattoo agent will use a registration code that will be traced back to you should your animal be picked up as a lost pet.

6. The tattoo agent will register your cat's code with Tatoo-A-Pet. You can now use the 1-800-TATTOOS as the phone number on your cat collar instead of your home phone number if you want. Tatoo-A-Pet will also provide identification tags for a small fee.

## WHAT NOT TO BUY WHEN OWNING CATS

Avoid furniture with rough fabric such as tapestry or wicker. Roughness will tempt cats to scratch. Velours are slippery and not so easy to snag. If you are unsure how the fabric of a new sofa will stand up to snags, get a sample of it, take it home and try to destroy. If you can snag it by stroking it with a wire brush or steel nails, it's probably not a wise purchase.

Cats can also easily destroy are terry cloth bath robes, foam rubber, dried flower arrangements, grassy house plants, sheer drapes and feathered ornament plants.

## CAT FOOD CONTACT LIST

Breeder's Choice Pet Foods, makers of Avo-Cat and Advance Pet Diets (APD). Canned and dry pet foods. 1-800-255-4AVO

Felidae, All Natural Cat & Kitten Formula. Dry and canned. 1-800-398-1600

Flint River Ranch Cat and Kitten food. Holistic veterinarians might carry this food. 1243 Columbia Ave, B-6, Riverside CA 92507.  909-682-5048

Lick Your Chops. Naturally preserved pet food. Also makers of Here's The Scoop Clumping Litter. 1-800-LI CHOPS (542-4677)

Natures Recipe, makes wide varieties of canned and dry pet food. Also carries a prescription formula for urinary tract problems.  1-800-237-3856

Neura & Old Mother Hubbard. Old Mother Hubbard makes canned food. Nuera Special Diet is a dry food designed for urinary tract problems. 1-800-225-0904

One Earth. Pet food. 1-800-8-EARTHY (832-7849)

PetGuard makes canned and dry pet food. 1-800-874-3221

Precise makes canned and dry food. 1-800-446-7148

Spots Stew, Manufactured for Halo Purely for Pets, 3433 East Lake Rd. Suite 14, Palm Harbor, FL 34684. Hearty canned stew for cats.  813-854-2214

Wysong has information, food supplements and different varieties of canned and dry food, including a formula for urinary tract problems. Wysong Corporation, 1880 N. Eastman, Midland, MI 48640. 1-800-748-0188

### CAT LITTERS CONTACT LIST

These litters were mentioned in chapters concerning litter and are found in many pet stores.

CatWorks, The Premium Cat Litter
  Absorption Corp.
  1051 Hilton Avenue
  Bellingham, WA 98225
  1-800-242-CATS (242-2287)

Cobby Cat
  Packaged by Sun See Company, Inc
  Box 33
  Bowling Green, OH 43402

Here's The Scoop Clumping Litter
  Integrated Pet Foods, Inc.
  610 Jeffers Cr.
  Exton, PA 19341
  1-800-542-4677

Nature's Touch Cat Box Filler
  (100% natural, made from Aspen bark and wood)
  Gentle Touch Corporation
  1909 Vicki Lane
  Norfolk, NE 68701

SWHEAT SCOOP Wheat Litter
  Pet Care Systems, Inc.
  1-800-SWHEATS

## NEUTRALIZER PRODUCT LIST

These neutralizers are found at most pet stores, mail order and some hardware stores. Read the labels for instructions.

AOE Animal Odor Eliminator
  Thornell Corporation
  160 Wheelock Road
  Penfield, NY 14526
  (AOE can be put into a syringe and injected into the
   carpet pad.)

Mom's Odor Eliminator sacks
  (In Cats, Cats & More Cats catalog)
  1-800-708-CATS (708-2287)
  Item number: EM-2
  (Two 1-lb. neutralizing sacks that can be reused by expos-
  ing them to the sun.)

Nature's Miracle
  (found in most pet or hardware stores)
  Pets 'N People, Inc.
  930 Indian Peak Rd., Suite 215
  Rolling Hills Estates, CA 90274
  310-544-7125

Pet Preference
  Cats Claws
  Morrilton, AR 72110
  1-800-783-0977

## CAT BEHAVIORISTS

To find a cat behaviorist call your local animal shelter or pet store; they often know who is in the area. Or, ask your veterinarian or pet sitter. Also try the yellow pages under "Cat Products, Services." Here are two behaviorists that specialize in cats:

- Pam Johnson Bennett, author of *Twisted Whiskers* and other cat books. Call or write, P. O. Box 50511, Nashville, TN 37205, phone 615-780-3626. A very compassionate feline behaviorist; I've talked with her myself. She's a very nice lady.

- Kate Gamble, San Francisco, CA, 415-564-5555 (you must leave a message). Her greeting is informative and lasts several minutes.

## CAT BOOKS

### CAT HEALTH, CARE

*Dr. Pitcairn's Complete Guide to Natural Health for Dogs & Cats*, by Richard H. Pitcairn, D.V.M., Ph.D. and Susan Hubble Pitcairn, 1995. An excellent source of pet information.

*The Home Pet Vet Guide for Cats*, by Martin I. Green, 1980. First aid for injury/illness.

*The Natural Remedy Book for Dogs & Cats*, by Diane Stein, 1994. Uses nutrition, naturopathy, vitamins, minerals, herb, homeopath, acupuncture/pressure, flower essences.

*The New Natural Cat, A Complete Guide for Finicky Owners*, by Anitra Frazier with Norma Eckroate, 1990. Also known as "cat queen," she wrote the bible on cat care. An excellent source for solving cat ailments and sick cats at home. Has raw food advice too.

### CAT FOOD BOOKS

*The Cat Lover's Cookbook*, by Franki B. Papai, 1993. Cat food recipes.

*Cat Nips! Feline Cuisine*, by Rick and Martha Reynolds, 1992. Cat food recipes.

*Food Pets Die For, Shocking Facts About Pet Food*, by Ann N. Martin, 1997. Describes what goes into pet food. It IS truly shocking!

*The Healthy Cat and Dog, Natural Recipes using nutritious, economical foods and Good Advice for happier, healthier and more beautiful pets*, By Joan Harper, 1992.

*Pet Allergies, Remedies for an Epidemic*, by Alfred J. Plechner, DVM and Martin Zucker, 1986. The startling facts on why pets die before their time, or why they itch or have fleas and what you can do about it.

*Super-Nutrition for Animals (Birds, Too!)*, by Nina Anderson, Dr. Howard Peiper and Alicia McWatters, M.S., 1996. Help for solving problems through nutrition and raw food.

*Reigning Cats and Dogs, Good Nutrition Healthy Happy Animals*, by Pat McKay, 1992. Raw food diet book.

## CAT BEHAVIOR, TRICKS, TOYS

*Cats on the Couch, The Complete Guide for Loving and Caring for Your Cat*, by Carole C. Wilbourn, 1988. Wilbourn is a cat therapist who writes cat behavior articles for "Cat Fancy" magazine.

*The City Cat, How to Live Healthily and Happily with Your Indoor Pet*, by Roz Riddle, 1988. Helpful book for cats who are kept indoors only.

*Do Cats Need Shrinks?*, by Peter Neville, 1991. Cat behaviorist.

*Feral Friends*, by Audrey Boag. A guide for living with feral cats. Send $4.00 to Audrey Boag, P. O. Box 714, Conifer, CO 80433.

*How to Get Your Cat To Do What You Want*, by Warren Eckstein and Fay Eckstein, 1990. Cat behavior book.

*How to Toilet-Train Your Cat, 21 Days to a Litter-Free Home*, by Paul Kunkel, 1991. Has step-by-step procedure on how to train your cat to use a toilet.

*The Indoor Cat, How to Understand, Enjoy and Care for House Cats*, by Patricia Curtis, 1997.

*Show Biz Tricks for Cats, 30 Fun and Easy Tricks You Can Teach Your Cat.* by Anne Gordon with Steve Duno, 1996.

*Train Your Cat*, by Terry Jester, 1992. A great book for cat behavior problems.

*Twisted Whiskers, Solving Your Cat's Behavior Problems*, by Pam Johnson, 1994. Compassionate dealing with cat behavior problems, aggression, new babies in household.

*Understanding the Cat You Love*, by Mordecai Siegal, 1994. More good things about cat behavior.

*51 Ways to Entertain Your Housecat While You're Out*, by Stephanie Laland, 1994. Easy-to-make toys and games guaranteed to keep your pet busy and happy.

## CAT FACTS

*Cat Facts,* by Marcus Schneck and Jill Caravan, 1993. Do cats think? Why are cat athletes? Cat breeds.

*The Life, History and Magic of the Cat*, by Fernand Méry, 1978. A most delightful book on cats, and the role they have played in our world.

*Mystic Cats, A Celebration of Cat Magic and Feline Charm*, by Roni Jay, 1995. Cat history, magical beliefs, fascinating folklore.

*Natural Cats*, by Chris Madsen, 1997. Cat facts, behavior and tips.

*The Pottenger Cats, A Study on Nutrition*, by Francis M. Pottenger, Jr., M.D., 1995. Results of a 10-year study on cats showing different effects of raw and cooked diets.

*Understanding Cats, Their History, Nature, and Behavior*, by Roger Tabor, 1995. This book is a good all-around fact cat book. The video is great, too.

## PICTURE BOOKS

*CATS, A First Discovery Book*, Created by Gallimard Jeunesse and Pascale de Bourgoing, 1989. A wonderful little picture book for children.

*Eyewitness Books CAT, Discover the World of Cats in Close-up—Their Evolution, Behavior and Secret Lives*, by Juliet Clutton-Brock, 1991. Wonderful child or adult picture book. A video is also available.

*Eyewitness Handbooks CATS, The visual guide to more than 250 types of cats from around the world*, by David Alderton, 1992. Beautiful pictures of practically every cat.

## OTHER HELPFUL PEOPLE BOOKS AND MAGAZINES

People who own cats can get pretty stressed sometimes. I know I do. Managing cat stress is easier if we have the right tools and know-how. These are just a few publications that have helped me handle stress:

*How to Survive Modern Technology*, by Charles T. McGee, M.D., 1979. Little helpful hints that could save your life in this age of technology and diet.

*Nourishing Traditions, The Cookbook that Challenges Politically Correct Nutrition and the Diet Dictocrats*, by Sally Fallon, 1995. This book is an excellent book about nutrition for people.

Price Pottenger Foundation. This is a nonprofit organization about food quality for people. They carry books on diet and the Pottenger Cat Study book, too. To receive free information or current prices on membership, call 1-800-FOODS-4-U.

## LOCAL PET SUPPLY STORES/SERVICES

### PET STORES

Blue Hills Dog & Cat Shoppe
2255 Main Street. #17
Longmont, CO 80501
303-651-2955
fax: 303-651-2028

Blue Hills Dog & Cat Shoppe carries an excellent supply of commercially prepared, naturally preserved cat and dog foods, as well as supplies, treats and toys.

Animal Crackers Pet Center
2877 W. 28th Street
Boulder, CO 80301
303-402-0626

Aqua Imports
2690 28th Street
Boulder, CO 80301
303-444-6971

Bark Avenue
101 E. Chester Street
Lafayette, CO 80026
303-664-WOOF (664-9663)

Whiskers
300 Second Avenue
Niwot, CO 80544
303-652-8809

### SERVICES

Aunt Ivy's Pet Sitting: Louisville, Superior & Lafayette, Colorado. 303-666-5273

KC Pet Sitting: Boulder County, Colorado. 303-530-1599

Kim Todd, Ttouch Practitioner (Tellington Touch, a form of health care and alternative training for companion animals), P. O. Box 130, Niwot, CO 80544. 303-545-9289

# Epilogue

# *Everything I Need to Know About Cats, I Have Learned From People*

BY ANNIE BRUCE

Cats and people both enjoy good food and a warm bed,

    Being loved,

    Having fun,

    Getting attention.

We get along with some and not with others.

Our children safe and well-fed.

Our elderly need more help than the young.

Hating boredom.

Loving freedom.

First impressions are important.

Routine and habits make us feel secure.

Respect for those who respect us.

Some of us are overweight, some lean, some loving, some mean.

Like to feel superior or good at something.

Like getting new things.

Like to own things.

We'll do almost anything to get what we want.

    A view from a window,

    To sleep in sunlight,

    Fresh air.

We relish and surrender to touch and massage,

Stretching, health, being fit.

We learn from our mothers and fathers.          B.

We learn by watching and doing.          M

Laziness is to be enjoyed.          I

We care for the sick.          L

To smell.          To   C

To touch.                                                        m

To hear.                                              u          p.

To sense.                                        j

To taste.                              To

To show joy, to have joy, to be joyful, although,

Bad events affect us, too, like moving and changes.

Death of a friend or relative, hurts. . . hurts big time.

Separation from our buddies is a real drag.

When disabled we become depressed, frustrated, shy,

          and prone to illness and accidents.

If we get hurt we are more cautious next time.

If we've been hurt it takes longer to earn back our trust.

We will hide when we're afraid and come out when it's safe.

We don't like seeing the doctor, or the dentist.

When we are stressed, we'll show it sooner or later. . . same for when

          we eat badly or don't exercise.

We retreat when we feel inferior or that we don't belong.

We isolate ourselves when we are not feeling well.

Recovery is painful.

We don't enjoy being laughed at.

We challenge newcomers.

We don't consider others important if we're unimportant to them.

If we don't know how to communicate what we want, we snap out, yell or feel bad.

But all in all, we manage.  And we do our best to enjoy ourselves no

    matter what befalls us.

We enjoy recognition.

We feel like hugs sometimes and sometimes not.

We usually welcome company.

We take pride in the things we do well.

Our truest loves, we love unconditionally.

We like to contribute to our families.

We like to try new things and test our limits.

Our eyes show our pain, anger, delight and curiosity.


        Oh yeah. . . and most of all?

          We love to dance

        and sometimes sing.

# ACKNOWLEDGMENTS

This book would not be possible without the talent, assistance and dedication of many wonderful people. I am very grateful for your help, support and patience.

Neil Feineman contributed greatly to this book and my sanity. Neil graciously stepped in to help after I ran out of hope and resources. He got Josh, Pam, David and James on board. And helped write, edit and organize this project to completion. His patience, persistence and dedication were extra-ordinary. Neil's allergy to cats makes him all that more dedicated to getting the job done.

Josh Gunn deserves special recognition. He turned a draft into a manuscript. His rewriting changed the book from an unyielding conglomeration of data into a coherent collection of sensibly organized chapters.

Thanks to Stephanie Roth-Nelson for her scheduling, publishing efforts and enthusiasm. Her editing and organization of the initial draft were important building blocks in the book's production.

Pam Ferdinand provided her extraordinary copyediting skills and her intellect. Pam got the text consistent and taught me more about writing.

Huck C. Leeds donated his time and technical advice. Huck was supportive and helped me when I needed help. I will always remember that.

An extra special thanks to David Levine who designed the logo, style and cover. Dave has an incredible eye for detail. I really appreciate his advice.

Steve "Crusher" Bartlett helped with the styling and production of the book.

Sara Levine was very kind to draw the artwork. She interrupted her busy schedule to help me out.

James Riddle illustrated the sidebars. I like how he made Louie and Marvin look like they do in real life.

The cat photo on the cover was shot by Julie Houck of Corbis.

More than anyone else, my husband, Bruce Delaplain, knew how to get down to what I meant to say. His meticulous questions, reviews and edit were the most critical to fine-tuning this book. Bruce made dinners and washed dishes, read and typed whenever he wasn't at his other jobs.

Special recognition goes to Diane Oldfield. Diane taught me about pet food and the role diet plays in a cat's health and behavior. Diane played an important part in helping me develop these commonsense techniques for cat behavior.

Many have helped review portions of this book. Their input was invaluable. I'd like to thank Anupam Barlow, Celia Bennett, Kay Brakowski, Karen Chaffee, Dr. J. Douglas Courtley, DVM, Kathleen Geary, Constance Krupka, Esther Mechler, Barbara Piren, Jerrilyn Rooney, Kay Yellowhorse and Joy Matey-Yetman.

A special thanks needs to be made to the rest of my friends and support group: Sherri Brando-Mineni and Ken Mineni, Lisa and Sam Booker, Ying Chang, Yolanda Hagan, Catalina Hall, Jill Harrison, Dr. Kimberly Harrison, DVM, Marcia Hooper, Ken Jimenez, Mr. Jones, Karen Lerner, Francesca Militeau, David and LaVon Sonne, and Shana Wagner.

And a very, very special thanks to all the cat owners who have come to me for help. With each question you have taught me a little bit more about cats.

I apologize if I missed anyone. I didn't mean to.

# ABOUT THE AUTHOR

*Cats are dangerous companions for writers because cat watching is a near-perfect method of writing avoidance.*

—DAN GREENBURG

Annie Bruce was born in Detroit, Michigan, in 1955, the youngest of six children. Her family owned black cats throughout her childhood. Like her mother and grandmother, Annie has a particular fondness for black cats and has owned black male cats for almost four decades.

Annie attended Cass Technical High School in downtown Detroit and worked for 20 years as a computer operator. Her volunteer work with sick and abused cats took her to public fairs, where she talked to cat owners about their cats' problems. When Annie realized that many owners and cats were suffering unnecessary hardship and expense, she started a consulting business. That business in turn led to this book.

Annie now lives in Boulder, Colorado, with her husband, Bruce, and four gorgeous cats, Marvin-My-Man, Louie-Louie, Abraham Lincoln and Bob. When she's not talking about cats, she's enjoying friends, eating and hip-hop dance classes.

# Index

# INDEX

# ORDER FORM

To order copies of *Cat Be Good : A Commonsense Approach to Training Your Cat,* ISBN 0-9674062-0-X:

- Telephone orders: Call BookMasters Toll Free: **1-800-247-6553**
- Fax orders to BookMasters: 419-281-6883
- Postal orders: Mail form and payment to:
  BookMasters, Inc., P.O. 388, Ashland, OH 44805
- Or visit these web sites:
  www.goodcatswearblack.com
  www.bookmasters.com

|  | Total |
|---|---|
| **Quantity** _____ @ $15.00 each |  |
| **Tax** - Colorado residents add 4.2% each book ($0.63) <br>     - Ohio residents add 6.25% each book ($0.94) |  |
| **Shipping & Handling (book rate)** <br> $4.00 for the first book and $2.00 for each additional book |  |
| **Total** |  |

Please indicate payment method:
❏ Check or money order (make payable to BookMasters, Inc.)
❏ Visa     ❏ MasterCard     ❏ American Express    ❏ Discover

Card #_____ Exp Date _____

Signature _____

Name _____
Address _____
City, State, ZIP _____
Phone _____

# ORDER FORM

To order copies of *Cat Be Good : A Commonsense Approach to Training Your Cat,* ISBN 0-9674062-0-X:

- Telephone orders: Call BookMasters Toll Free: **1-800-247-6553**
- Fax orders to BookMasters: 419-281-6883
- Postal orders: Mail form and payment to:
    BookMasters, Inc., P.O. 388, Ashland, OH 44805
- Or visit these web sites:
    www.goodcatswearblack.com
    www.bookmasters.com

|  | *Total* |
|---|---|
| **Quantity** _____ @ $15.00 each |  |
| **Tax** - Colorado residents add 4.2% each book ($0.63)<br> - Ohio residents add 6.25% each book ($0.94) |  |
| **Shipping & Handling (book rate)**<br>$4.00 for the first book and $2.00 for each additional book |  |
| **Total** |  |

Please indicate payment method:
❏ Check or money order (make payable to BookMasters, Inc.)
❏ Visa    ❏ MasterCard    ❏ American Express    ❏ Discover

Card #_____ Exp Date _____

Signature _____

Name _____
Address _____
City, State, ZIP _____
Phone _____

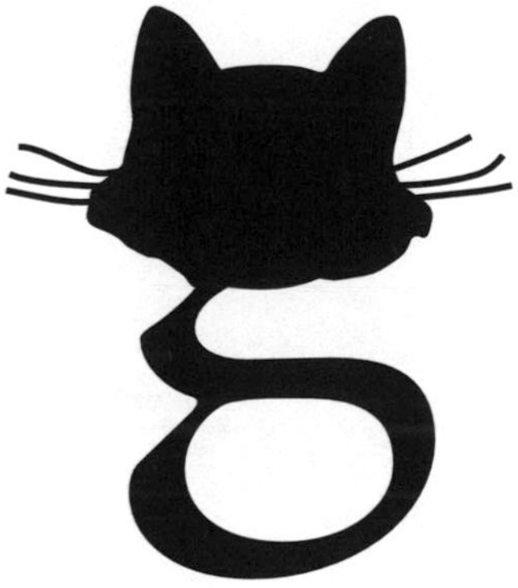